LET THE STUDENTS SPEAK!

A History of the Fight
for Free Expression
in American Schools

David L. Hudson Jr.

Let the People Speak
Christopher Finan, Series Editor

Beacon Press
Boston

Let the People Speak: Books about the Historical Battle for Our
Most Important Freedom. A series edited by Christopher Finan.

Beacon Press
25 Beacon Street
Boston, Massachusetts 02108-2892
www.beacon.org

Beacon Press books
are published under the auspices of
the Unitarian Universalist Association of Congregations.

14 13 12 11   8 7 6 5 4 3 2 1

This book is printed on acid-free paper that meets the uncoated paper
ANSI/NISO specifications for permanence as revised in 1992.

Text design by Wilsted & Taylor Publishing Services

Library of Congress Cataloging-in-Publication Data
Hudson, David L.
Let the students speak! : a history of the fight for free expression in
American schools / David L. Hudson Jr.
p. cm.
Includes bibliographical references and index.
ISBN 978-0-8070-4454-4 (pbk. : alk. paper) 1. Freedom of speech—
United States—Cases. 2. Freedom of expression—United States—
Cases. 3. United States. Constitution. 1st Amendment. 4. Students—
Civil rights—United States—Cases. I. Title.
KF4772.H83 2011
342.7308'53—dc22   2010050227

TO *Terry Morley, Janis Kyser, and David Fuqua*

Congress shall make no law respecting an establishment of religion, or prohibiting the free exercise thereof; or abridging the freedom of speech, or the press; or the right of the people peaceably to assemble, and to petition the Government for a redress of grievances.

—The First Amendment to the United States Constitution

That don't fly here, man.

—Public school student on the First Amendment in his school

CONTENTS

EDITOR'S NOTE

The American people take free speech for granted. Almost everyone knows that the First Amendment to the Constitution protects freedom of speech and freedom of the press. It is only natural to assume that Americans have always enjoyed the freedom to say what we want, when and where we want. It follows that we really don't have to worry about free speech. It is something built into our system of government.

But there has always been censorship in the United States. In the beginning, there was so little understanding of the meaning of free speech that just a few years after the adoption of the First Amendment some of the Founding Fathers passed the Alien and Sedition Acts and jailed people who criticized the government. Throughout the nineteenth century, Americans turned a blind eye to the suppression of groups advocating what were then outrageous ideas: abolitionists who called for an end to slavery were attacked by mobs and denied the right to present their petitions to Congress; and "sex radicals" who demanded equal rights for women were prosecuted for obscenity under the Comstock Act, the first federal censorship law. Workers trying to organize unions were the largest group to suffer. They were routinely denied meeting places, and when they tried to strike they confronted sweeping injunctions that banned picketing, orders that were often violently enforced by police and hired thugs.

It was only in the twentieth century that the First Amendment really began to mean something. The prosecution of more than two thousand Americans for speaking against United States participation in World War I convinced a small group of men and women that free speech must be protected. "When men have realized that time has upset many fighting faiths, they may come to believe . . . that the ultimate good desired is better reached by free trade in ideas," Supreme Court justice Oliver Wendell Holmes wrote in a 1919 legal opinion criticizing the conviction of several war protesters. The American Civil Liberties Union was founded in 1920 to lead the fight for free speech. Finally, in 1931, the Supreme Court issued its first decisions protecting free speech. Despite some setbacks, mostly during wartime, protections for free speech have grown strongly over the last eighty years.

This does not mean that the fight for free speech is over. There are more battles over free speech today than ever. Government has a natural tendency toward secrecy and suppression. In addition, the very freedom with which we now express ourselves has caused some to complain that we have gone too far in protecting speech and led them to support repressive legislation. But the ACLU is no longer alone. Today there are dozens of groups defending First Amendment rights.

Let the People Speak: Books about the Historical Battle for Our Most Important Freedom is a series about the origins and growth of free speech in the United States. We hope that it will provide a background for understanding current controversies and help build support for those who are fighting for free speech. The inaugural volume, David Hudson's book about free speech in public schools, shows that despite the growth of their First Amendment rights, students still face significant restrictions on their ability to speak freely. It explains why the fight for free speech must continue.

Christopher Finan
Series Editor
Let the People Speak

INTRODUCTION

The First Amendment—the first forty-five words of the Bill of Rights in the United States Constitution—reads in stark terms: "Congress shall make no law . . . abridging the freedom of speech." United States Supreme Court decisions eventually established that the "first freedom" applied to more than Congress. This meant and still means that the First Amendment limits the power of any government official—federal, state, or local—to punish individuals for their expression. It covers not only members of Congress but also the president of the United States, state officials, mayors, police officers, and public school administrators. At least that is the ideal.

Many public school students know better. They experience firsthand an environment that does not promote their free expression. They sense that the ideal doesn't match the reality. The First Amendment is not a high priority at their schools.

In part this is understandable. School officials face the daunting task of providing a safe place for students to learn. They are responsible for the well-being of the young people that come through their doors. They face the danger of mass school shootings, such as the infamous attack at Columbine that seared the nation's collective conscience. They confront new dimensions of expression in the Internet and cyberbullying—a form of online harassment that has attracted the attention of federal and state lawmakers. Officials in some school districts face the insidious spread of gang influence and violence.

Furthermore, context affects the First Amendment. An adult citizen has broad license to criticize the police, but a police officer has less freedom to criticize his sergeant. A minor has greater free speech rights when strolling down a public street than when walking down the school hallway. The Supreme Court has explained that student rights must be evaluated according to the "special characteristics of the school environment."

This book examines that special environment, focusing on the conflict between school authority and student speech rights. It's a rich history filled with stories of individual students who clashed with school officials, sometimes winning and sometimes losing.

Consider briefly the case of Jeffrey and Jonathan Pyle, two high school students from Massachusetts whose free speech controversy inspired them both to become lawyers. The brothers' lesson about the fragility of First Amendment freedoms in school occurred in 1993, after they wore T-shirts to school that irked officials at South Hadley Public High School. Jeffrey, a senior and a member of the school band and the drama club, wore a shirt to gym class that read: CO-ED NAKED BAND: DO IT TO THE RHYTHM. His younger brother Jonathan, a sophomore, wore a shirt with the message: SEE DICK DRINK. SEE DICK DRIVE. SEE DICK DIE. DON'T BE A DICK!

The principal called them into his office and eventually accused them of insubordination when they refused to remove the shirts. Jeffrey and Jonathan—with help from their father, Christopher, who taught constitutional law at Mount Holyoke College—sued in federal court challenging their school's dress code. They contended that the parts of the code banning vulgar language violated the First Amendment and a Massachusetts state law that provided even more free speech protection. In the wake of a restrictive 1988 Supreme Court decision (*Hazelwood School District v. Kuhlmeier*) limiting student rights, the Massachusetts legislature had responded by amending a 1974 state law regarding student expression. That 1974 law had given school districts the option of providing public school students with strong free speech protections. In July 1988—six months after the Supreme Court's decision—the Massachusetts legislature amended its law and made it mandatory for school districts. The law stipulates that public school officials cannot punish students for their expression unless the student speech is disruptive.

The Pyles' case came before U.S. district judge Michael Ponser, who held a four-day hearing on the T-shirts. "The First Amendment does not permit official repression or homogenization of ideas, even odious ideas, and even when the expression of these ideas may result in hurt feelings or a sense of being harassed," Ponser wrote in *Pyle v. South Hadley School Committee* (1993). This meant that the harassment provision of the South Hadley dress code was history.

However, Judge Ponser upheld the part of the dress code that allowed school officials to limit vulgar student speech. The Pyle brothers appealed that portion of the ruling to a higher court—the U.S. Court of Appeals for the First Circuit, which meets in Boston. The First Circuit then sent a question of law—called a certified question—to the state supreme court, asking:

> Do high school students in public schools have the freedom under . . . [state law] . . . to engage in non-school-sponsored expression that may reasonably be considered vulgar, but causes no disruption or disorder?

The Supreme Judicial Court of Massachusetts answered yes and ruled in favor of the Pyle brothers in July 1996. "Our Legislature is free to grant greater rights to the citizens of this Commonwealth than would otherwise be protected under the United States Constitution," the court proclaimed. Massachusetts law established that students had the right to freedom of expression unless the speech caused "disruption or disorder within the school." The Pyles' shirts—even if school officials viewed them as obnoxious and irreverent—caused no significant disruption at South Hadley.

The net result was that Jeffrey and Jonathan Pyle won their case. Their experience as student litigants inspired them to become lawyers, as both graduated from prestigious law schools and are practicing attorneys. "I like to say that my life path was charted by my choice of T-shirt on my way to gym class," says Jeffrey, who practices First Amendment law in Massachusetts.

When the Massachusetts high court decision came out, Jeffrey was close to graduating from Trinity College. "I thought to myself, 'Hell, I'll just apply to law school.'" He graduated from Boston College Law School and then accepted a judicial clerkship from none other than Judge Michael Ponser—the judge who had ruled in his T-shirt case years earlier. "We had a somewhat different view of the First Amendment but he was a great judge and I learned much from the experience." Now, Pyle practices law in the area, sometimes serving as a volunteer attorney for the Massachusetts American Civil Liberties Union (ACLU) and speaking to young students about the First Amendment.

Jeffrey Pyle is not alone in finding out that censorship is alive and well in public schools in the United States. Students often face discipline for violating dress codes, posting inappropriate material on the Internet, writing controversial stories in school newspapers, and penning violent-themed material for class assignments. In an age of zero tolerance, school officials often have little respect for student expression that pushes boundaries or tests limits.

The story of the Pyle brothers is just one of many. The history of student expression is a turbulent one marked by highs and lows. Early student speech cases show that school officials had complete command over students, akin to a master–slave relationship. But times change and laws evolve.

The history of student expression also is a rich one, involving religious minorities, civil rights activists, war protesters, and others who simply wanted to be different with their choice of hair style, T-shirt message, or tattoo. It involves flag salutes, freedom buttons, black armbands, and school newspaper articles. Most importantly, the history of student expression involves young people, who are the future of our constitutional democracy. Many of them study in school environments that discourage individuality and demand conformity. Students learn the grand words of the First Amendment—"Congress shall make no law . . . abridging the freedom of speech"—but live in a world where their speech is controlled and sometimes their voices are silenced.

Many advocates fear that students will not appreciate the value of the First Amendment if they don't experience its benefits while in school. U.S. Supreme Court justice Robert Jackson warned of this more than sixty-five years ago: "That they are educating the young for citizenship is reason for scrupulous protection of Constitutional freedoms of the individual, if we are not to strangle the free mind at its source and teach youth to discount important principles of our government as mere platitudes."

Let the story of student expression begin.

CHAPTER 1

NO RIGHTS FOR STUDENTS

In 2007, Clarence Thomas broke ranks with his colleagues on the U.S. Supreme Court when deciding an unusual case officially named *Morse v. Frederick*. The case began after a high school principal in Alaska suspended a student for unfurling a provocative banner near school with the strange message BONG HITS 4 JESUS. (Much more on this fascinating case later.)

Eight members of the Court debated whether the student had a First Amendment *right* to display his cryptic message. They disagreed over the meaning of "Bong Hits 4 Jesus" and the outcome of the case, but they all paid homage to past Supreme Court cases clearly establishing that students have free speech rights in school. The justices did this for good reason, because nearly forty years ago the Court had stated in *Tinker v. Des Moines Independent Community School District* (1969), "It can hardly be argued that . . . students . . . shed their constitutional rights to freedom of speech or expression at the schoolhouse gate." To eight members of the Court in 2007, *Tinker* was the seminal student speech case. It was the law.

Thomas disagreed, finding that students should have no free speech rights. He did so because of his belief in a constitutional doctrine called originalism. Originalists interpret the Constitution and the Bill of Rights by focusing on the meaning they believe those words had for the Founding Fathers—the individuals who created the Constitution and the Bill of Rights in 1787 and 1791 respectively. In legal terms, Thomas focused on the "original intent" of the Founding Fathers. Drawing on that theory, Thomas boldly proclaimed in his separate opinion: "As originally understood, the Constitution does not afford students a right to free speech in public schools." Thomas said that the Court should overrule *Tinker*, consigning it to the dustbin of history.

To support his position, Thomas engaged in a historical analysis of public schools during the course of the nineteenth century. He surveyed the relatively few published decisions from cases in which students had contested punishments meted out to them by school officials. As Thomas correctly noted, the courts ruled against these students the vast majority of the time. To these courts, the First Amendment was an afterthought and the concept of student rights was foreign.

"Early public schools gave total control to teachers, who expected obedience and respect from students," Thomas wrote. "And courts routinely deferred to schools' authority to make rules and to discipline students for violating those rules." While his colleagues focused on *Tinker* and subsequent decisions by the Court, Thomas argued that the Supreme Court had usurped the authority of school officials. Thomas focused on earlier student speech cases that showed courts deferring to the authority of school officials. Among the many cases he cited was a mid-nineteenth-century opinion by the Vermont Supreme Court called *Lander v. Seaver* (1859).

MAKING FUN OF THE TEACHER

In 1858, eleven-year-old Peter Lander Jr. received a rawhide whipping from his teacher, A. B. Seaver, after the Burlington, Vermont, youth used "saucy and disrespectful" language to the teacher after school. Lander was driving his father's cows a couple of hours after school when he passed schoolmaster Seaver's house. The impetuous Lander had the temerity to shout at his teacher "Old Jack Seaver!" in the presence of other students.

The next day Seaver exacted his revenge by beating Lander with a small rawhide. Lander and his father alleged that Seaver violated the law by exacting excessive corporal punishment. The Landers contended that the teacher had no authority to punish Peter for conduct that occurred off school grounds. They reasoned that it was a matter of parental, not school, discipline. The Vermont Supreme Court disagreed, finding that Seaver's conduct was not clearly excessive and fell within the broad range of authority given schoolmasters to dole out punishments that would have the effect of keeping order in school. Given that the concept of student speech rights did not exist, the outcome of Lander's case hinged on whether his punishment was excessive. For courts in 1859, a beating with rawhide for insulting an authority figure seemed reasonable. Happily, courts today wouldn't agree.

The more interesting part of the analysis concerned the question of whether Seaver had the authority to punish Lander for conduct or misconduct committed outside of school. The Vermont Supreme Court determined that student misconduct "must not have merely a remote and indirect tendency to injure the school." Otherwise, the matter is for the parents, "and they alone have the power of punishment."

The court then identified a point that modern-day school officials, school boards, and judges still grapple with every day—how to determine when off-campus student expression or expressive conduct has a direct enough connection to school activities to merit discipline. "It will often be difficult to distinguish between the acts which have such an immediate and those which have such a remote tendency," the Vermont high court said. "Hence each case must be determined by its peculiar circumstances."

Unfortunately for Peter Lander, the Vermont court determined that his "Old Jack Seaver" comment had a direct, rather than remote, connection. The court explained that schoolmasters must have the power to discipline students for "language used to other scholars to stir up disorder and insubordination or to heap odium and disgrace upon the master." Schoolmasters "by common consent . . . and universal custom" have the power to prohibit such language, because "such power is essential to the preservation of order, decency, decorum and good government in schools."

WHISTLEBLOWER

In explaining that students had no rights, Justice Clarence Thomas specifically cited not only the "Old Jack Seaver" case, but also a case involving a student who raised a school safety issue in *Wooster v. Sunderland* (1915). In 1913, in the spring of his senior year, Earl Wooster, a public high school student in Fresno, California, learned the hard way that students possessed few rights. While a student at Fresno High School, Wooster had learned the ropes of the newspaper industry from the legendary editor of the *Fresno Morning Republican*, Chester Harvey Rowell. Wooster first worked as a delivery boy and then as a mailroom clerk. Perhaps his experience at a publication devoted to free expression inspired Wooster to believe in his own right to speak out against perceived abuses. Perhaps working under the tutelage of Rowell, a leader of the so-called "Republican progressives," also moved Wooster to appreciate the value of speech as an engine of social change.

Not only did Wooster acquire an appreciation for free expression, he also learned the value of hard work, as he balanced school and work. He went to school during the day and then worked at the paper at night, sometimes arriving at work at 2:00 a.m. for cleaning duties. In an oral history published by the University of Nevada, Wooster admitted that "I was no angel in any sense," but he developed a strong work ethic and sense of right and wrong—and he would not back down if people in authority were wrong.

Wooster's willingness to stand up for what he believed landed him in conflict with school officials at Fresno High. A group of students had decided to have what Wooster termed an "interclass fight." He recalled that such fights "were really very asinine, but they were very dear to the hearts of the students—both girls and boys." However, school officials weren't so enamored of student fights. They learned about the planned fight and ordered students not to participate. This upset many students and five students responded by driving to the house of the principal, Mr. Frederick Liddeke, and chanting, "To hell with Liddeke."

Liddeke, who had come to admire Wooster for his candor on

other school matters during the year, questioned the student about the incident. Wooster truthfully denied that he had participated in principal bashing. School officials then called a meeting of the entire student body to discuss the situation and why they had interceded to stop the fight. At the meeting, Wooster stood up before the student body to make the striking observation that "if the school board was so interested in keeping the bones of the students from being broken, probably they'd put some fire exits on the assembly hall."

In other words, Wooster made the valid point that if school officials were going to express concern about student safety, perhaps they should pay attention to fire codes in the gymnasium and the chemistry room. A local newspaper printed Wooster's speech, drawing unflattering attention to student discipline and fire safety problems. As Wooster recalled in his memoir, some school officials became so incensed that they later pulled him off the stage during a Shakespearean play he was performing at the school. The officials ordered Wooster, still dressed in his costume from the play, to retract his critical comments. Earl adamantly refused to do so. Why, he thought, should he apologize for speaking the truth?

During an interview years later, Wooster said that if school officials had told him they were they were planning to place fire escapes in the assembly hall, he would have apologized. Instead, he believed school officials treated him poorly. After he refused to take back his critical comments, the school board in Fresno suspended him.

"It created a terrific furor in the community, and the night of graduation, they almost had a riot when they gave out unsigned diplomas to the students," Wooster recalled. School officials had decided to expel him and withhold his diploma until he apologized. They also told Wooster to address the school board and explain his actions. He attended the meeting and explained his position. He admitted that his speech "was intended as a slam" against the school officials.

Attorney E. A. Williams offered to represent Wooster and his father, filing a lawsuit against the school board for withholding Earl's diploma. The lawsuit contended that the actions of the school board were unreasonable. Trial judge H. Z. Austin rejected Wooster's arguments and sided with school officials.

Determined to continue, Wooster appealed the trial court's decision to the California Court of Appeals. On March 15, 1915, the appeals court issued its opinion in *Wooster v. Sunderland*, affirming the trial judge's ruling. The appellate court wrote at length about the duty of students to exercise proper deportment and fulfill the "obligation of obedience to lawful commands."

The appellate court found that Wooster had delivered his "incendiary address" in a "caustic" manner and that it had the effect of "creating in the minds of the students a spirit of insubordination and was subversive of the good order and discipline of the school." Schools could punish students who intended to foment disrespect among their peers toward school officials, the court reasoned.

The appeals court focused on the legal argument that expulsion was too harsh a remedy for Wooster's speech about potential safety problems in the school. Though the court acknowledged that the penalty bordered on the extreme, it still sided with school officials. "In the present case an apology would have been adequate punishment for the misconduct," the court wrote, but Wooster's refusal to make an apology "not only accentuated his misconduct but made it necessary for the defendants to resort to an order of expulsion."

Modern readers might find it remarkable that the California appeals court failed to mention the First Amendment, freedom of speech, or freedom of expression. The entire opinion instead focused on the authority of the school board, the duty of students to obey, and the reasonableness of the punishment. The opinion largely ignored the fact that Wooster was a whistleblower of sorts. The court didn't address the content of his speech and didn't address whether his warnings about possible fires and safety were true or false. Instead, the opinion focused on the authority of school officials and reasonableness of punishment. That explains why Justice Thomas found it an appealing precedent to cite for his declaration that students should have no First Amendment rights.

THE LIPSTICK WAR

Earl Wooster was not the only young person who dared to stand toe to toe with school officials at a time when students had few, if any, rights. Often seen as the progenitor of modern challengers to school dress codes, seventeen-year-old Pearl Pugsley from Knobel, Arkansas, filed a lawsuit in 1921 that made national news, including a story in the *New York Times*. In September, the Knobel School Board had passed the following rule: "The wearing of transparent hosiery, low-necked dresses and any style of clothing tending to immodesty in dress, or the use of face powder or cosmetics, is prohibited." School officials said they needed to ban short skirts and cosmetics because such items tended to "distract" the boys and keep them from focusing upon their studies.

Such a move in modern-day American high schools might start a riot or a revolution, or at a minimum Facebook postings blasting school officials for a ridiculous rule. But in Knobel, only "little Pearl Pugsley"—dubbed by one newspaper writer as the "Joan De Arc of the Lipstick War"—was bold enough to challenge the rule.

It has been said that "well-behaved women seldom make history." Pearl Pugsley made history. According to the *New York Times*, after reading the rule, she defiantly "daubed more powder on her cheeks." A teacher ordered her to go home and wash her face. Principal N. E. Hicks supported the teacher. When Pugsley continued to defy the rule, Hicks took the matter to the school board. The school board backed Hicks and expelled Pugsley.

She went home but didn't stay there, as she and her father proceeded to a lawyer's office, where she promptly filed a lawsuit challenging the rule. "It wasn't a desire to create trouble when the suit was brought," Pugsley said. "I merely felt that my toes were being trampled on, so to speak, and the Irish blood in me began to boil." She declared that she would "fight the case to a finish." Her resolve was buoyed by thousands of encouraging letters she received from supporters.

The case came before Judge W. W. Bandy, who agreed that the rule against lipstick was unreasonable. However, he would not order

school officials to readmit Pugsley. He believed the matter was up to the discretion of the school board and that the courts should not interfere with the day-to-day decisions of the schools. Honoring the wishes of her then-dying father, Pugsley took the case all the way to the Arkansas Supreme Court, where she lost by a 2–1 vote in *Pugsley v. Sellmeyer* (1923). The judges in the majority not only ruled in favor of school officials but also determined that the rule was reasonable. They believed the rule was not arbitrary and that courts should be hesitant to interfere with the functioning of the school. "It will be remembered that respect for constitutional authority . . . is an essential lesson to qualify one for duties of citizenship, and that the schoolroom is an appropriate place to teach that lesson," the majority wrote, adding that the "courts should hesitate to substitute their own will and judgment for that of the school boards."

Pearl Pugsley did earn the vote of one Arkansas Supreme Court justice—Jesse C. Hart, who found the rule "unreasonable and beyond the exercise of discretion." He wrote in memorable language: "'Useless laws diminish the authority of necessary ones.' The tone of the majority opinion exemplifies the wisdom of this old proverb."

Pearl Pugsley may have lost in court but she earned the admiration of people across the country. Her battle also led school officials to rescind the lipstick ban.

LAMPOONING POEM AND INSULTING ESSAY

Other students learned you dare not write words that school officials deem threatening to authority or insolent to school officials. In 1908, the Wisconsin Supreme Court decided a case—*State ex rel. Dresser v. District Board*—that involved two sisters and a poem. A senior at the high school in St. Croix Falls, Wisconsin, had written a poem mocking school rules and satirizing a teacher. The Dresser sisters took their classmate's poem to the local newspaper for publication.

The paper published the poem, causing consternation on the part of school officials, who believed that the work engendered disrespect among other students and the community. For submitting the poem to the newspapers, the two sisters were expelled by Principal

G. J. Baker, who believed that the poem exposed teachers to contempt and ridicule. Baker alleged that the poem caused "defiance toward the proper control and management of the school."

The Dresser sisters sued, seeking reinstatement to school. Principal Baker told the girls they could not come back to school until they apologized and paid forty cents each. On December 1906, a juvenile referee upheld the principal's decision and rejected the sisters' claims. A Wisconsin trial judge adopted the referee's findings and upheld the expulsion of the Dresser sisters. On appeal, the Wisconsin Supreme Court affirmed not only the lower court decision but also waxed at length about the broad powers of school officials.

Much as Peter Lander's lawyer did fifty years earlier, the attorney for the Dresser sisters contended that the school lacked the authority to punish a student for material created off campus. If anything, the matter required parental, not school, discipline. However, the Wisconsin Supreme Court made clear that it was not in a position to determine whether the school officials initiated an appropriate punishment. "We are not called upon to approve the practical wisdom displayed by the school authorities in dealing with the hasty conduct of thoughtless school children," the court wrote, reasoning that "school authorities have the power to suspend a pupil for an offense committed outside of school hours and not in the presence of the teacher which has a direct and immediate tendency to influence the conduct of the teachers, and to bring them into ridicule and contempt." According to the court, "such power is essential to the preservation of order, decency, decorum, and good government in the public schools."

The Wisconsin Supreme Court found that school officials' power could extend to off-campus speech, particularly when such speech would affect other members of the school community, including students, teachers, and administrators. The court accepted Principal Baker's argument that the poem could cause other students to question school officials and lead to a breakdown of discipline in the school.

The opinion also illustrated the mentality of the courts in the early twentieth century as to the near-complete control of school authorities over children. The court even used the term *master* when referring to the school officials. The Wisconsin court spoke of the students' "obligations of obedience to lawful commands, subordination, civil deportment, respect for the rights of other pupils and fidelity to duty."

The reality was that the teacher–student and school official–student relationship was akin to the severely applied master–servant relationship in employment law of the day. In employment law, what the employer said was the law of the land. The same principle applied in schools. Employees and students were servants with little to no legal recourse. The *Dresser* court ruling also made a point that echoes in the twenty-first century, as courts continue to grapple with questions as to the reach of school officials' authority. School officials today struggle with whether they have the power to restrict off-campus student expression online on the students' own computers, cell phones, or other mobile devices.

Unlike the Dresser sisters, Camilla G. Booth of Covington, Kentucky, landed in hot water for an assigned project—an in-class essay. English teacher Ella Shay deemed Booth's essay not only unsuitable but also a direct insult to Shay and her position. She reported Booth to school authorities, who expelled her. Booth and her father filed a lawsuit in Kenton Circuit Court, seeking an order compelling the Covington School Board to allow Camilla to return to school. A circuit court granted her motion, agreeing that the school board had exceeded its power in expelling her.

School officials quickly appealed to the Kentucky Court of Appeals, which reversed the lower court's decision and ruled in favor of the school officials. Judge B. L. D. Guffy of Morgantown authored the opinion. Guffy was a well-respected jurist said to resemble Abraham Lincoln. Former Kentucky governor and U.S. senator William O'Connell Bradley characterized Judge Guffy in his writings as "a most eccentric and original character."

Yet Guffy was not eccentric in his handling of school law cases; in fact, he would be quite conventional in deferring to the authority of school officials in Camilla Booth's case. Guffy acknowledged that Booth may not have meant to insult Shay, but he reasoned that it was enough that the superintendent of the school system and the board of education had considered it "grossly insulting." Remarkably, Guffy's opinion in *Board of Education v. Booth* (1901) never mentions the content of Booth's essay. Today, when courts consider a student's expulsion for an essay or Internet posting, they quote the student's work. But Judge Guffy never provided the text of Booth's essay or even quoted the allegedly "grossly insulting" language. In his view, it was enough that school officials were "better qualified" to determine the appropriate level of discipline.

CONTROLLING STUDENT GROUP EXPRESSION

The judicial mindset of deferring to school officials extended beyond individual student expression to certain forms of collective activity. Some courts, for example, in the early twentieth century upheld school rules prohibiting school recognition of so-called "secret societies"—progenitors of modern-day fraternities and sororities.

The Chicago Board of Education, for one, actively sought to eliminate the influences of fraternities and sororities in public education. With the overall increase in the number of public school students, including a sharp rise in the number of immigrants, school officials adhered to the Progressive idea that school environments should be free from class distinctions. A few years earlier, in 1904, the board passed a rule denying official recognition to any fraternity or sorority by public schools. It also provided that no student who was a member of any such "secret society" would be permitted to represent the school in any athletic or literary competition. In 1907, the Board of Education laid out its position on secret societies: "The American common school system stands for equal opportunities for all pupils to get a preparation for the responsibilities that come with maturity. Any influence that disturbs this equality of opportunity disturbs the spirit and destroys the basic purpose of our common schools."

Eberle L. Wilson, a member of the Phi Sigma fraternity and a student at Hyde Park High School, challenged the rule in an Illinois state court. After a trial court upheld the rule, Wilson appealed to the Illinois Court of Appeals, which affirmed the lower court's decision in *Wilson v. Board of Education of the City of Chicago* (1908). The appeals court determined that the prohibition against school recognition of such clubs was reasonable, as giving official sanction to such groups "would be the recognition of a class distinction contrary to the fundamental spirit of our laws." The court concluded: "But for the power of the Board of Education to make and enforce reasonable disciplinary rules, the orderly control of the conduct of the pupils would be impossible."

Today, the First Amendment and a federal law called the Equal Access Act provide protection for many student groups. Schools generally cannot regulate outside activities or group memberships of students. They cannot condition participation in student extracurricular groups based on membership in outside civic organizations.

ALL ABOUT REASONABLENESS

All of the student litigants—Peter Lander, Earl Wooster, Pearl Pugsley, the Dresser sisters, Camilla Booth, and Eberle Wilson —challenged school officials' authority to discipline them for forms of expression or expressive activity arguably covered by the First Amendment. But in their arguments the First Amendment wasn't discussed or even mentioned. Instead, the judicial decisions of the nineteenth and early twentieth centuries center on whether school authority exceeded the broad boundaries of reasonableness.

Only when a school official's action could be characterized as being beyond all bounds of reasonableness would the student have a chance. One rare example of a high school student who beat the odds was Beth Valentine in Casey, Iowa. In May 1918, Valentine had met all the requirements for graduation but refused to wear a cap and gown for the ceremony because she believed that the caps and gowns—worn by many students through the years—were not sanitary. The gowns had been fumigated with formaldehyde and smelled horrible. Valentine refused to wear one. Her physician had advised her that the disinfectant used by the school officials would not make the caps and gowns free from the possibility of transmitting a contagious disease.

When she refused to wear the cap and gown, the school withheld her diploma, and she sued. School officials prevailed in the lower court, but the Iowa Supreme Court reversed the decision and ruled in her favor. The Iowa high court in *Valentine v. Independent School District of Casey* (1919) classified the ruling barring Valentine from obtaining her diploma as "unreasonable and arbitrary." It took another ruling by the same court two years later to force the school to give her the diploma.

Around the same time, in Oklahoma, a school principal named Billingsley, who also served as a teacher, filled out a register of daily attendance and grades of his students. Next to the name of student Wallace Dawkins, Billingsley wrote: "Drag [likely a local term for intoxicated] all the time. Ruined by tobacco and whisky." Billingsley gave the register to a school clerk, who showed it to various members of the public. Dawkins and his father were not happy to learn about Billingsley's snide notation. An attorney for Dawkins sued, introducing evidence that Dawkins was a "boy of good habits" who did not drink whiskey. Though a trial court ruled in favor of Billingsley, the Oklahoma Supreme Court reversed the ruling, finding that the evidence "clearly established that the words written by the defendant . . . were defamatory . . . and sufficient to take the case to a jury."

The *Valentine* and *Dawkins* examples showed that on occasion a court would find the actions of school officials so far beyond the pale of reasonableness that it would respect the rights of students. But these cases were the exception, not the rule.

RISING NUMBER OF SCHOOLS, FEW FREE SPEECH CHALLENGES

From the creation of public schools until well into the first half of the twentieth century, very few students and parents dared challenge school officials. An important shift was taking place, though, as the number of public schools exploded exponentially in the late nineteenth and early twentieth centuries with some scholars estimating an increase as high as 700 percent. Such rapid growth led to an increase in rules and regulations needed to control a larger number of students. Significantly, it would also lead to more challenges of school rules by students and their parents.

This new wave of challenges by students rarely if ever involved the First Amendment or corresponding free expression provisions of state constitutions. In part, this dearth of free speech claims occurred because the U.S. Supreme Court had not yet developed a body of First Amendment law. It would take the cataclysmic event of World War I, when Congress began passing laws to punish political dissidents—Communists, anarchists, Socialists, and others whom political leaders feared would upset the U.S. war effort—for the high court to turn its attention to the First Amendment. But, the lack of First Amendment claims also occurred for a more technical legal reason. The text of the First Amendment provides that "Congress shall make no law . . . abridging the freedom of speech." In the early twentieth century, the provisions of the Bill of Rights, including the First Amendment, only protected people from infringement by the federal government, including the U.S. Congress. The First Amendment did not at that point protect people—including students—from infringements by state and local government officials. A local teacher was not Congress within the meaning of "Congress shall make no law."

It took the passage of the Fourteenth Amendment in 1868 and Supreme Court decisions beginning in 1925 for the courts to apply the First Amendment in cases involving state and local government officials. The vehicle by which the Court drove the First Amendment to the state and local governments was the Due Process Clause of the Fourteenth Amendment—"no state shall deny any person life, liberty or property without due process of law." Simply stated, the U.S. Supreme Court in *Gitlow v. New York* (1925) determined that freedom of speech was a part of "liberty" in the Due Process Clause.

This means that when a school official today punishes a student for his or her speech, the First Amendment applies. It did not apply in Earl Wooster's—or Camilla Booth's—time.

The rule of reasonableness also applied because state and federal courts were not always sensitive to the question of individual rights like freedom of speech—and neither was the U.S. Supreme Court. Technically, state courts could have applied free speech provisions of their state constitutions to protect students. But they didn't. Lawyers didn't even raise these state constitutional law claims. The legal system was more concerned with the protection of property rights than individual rights. Of course, the other reality was that courts simply didn't care about protecting "student rights."

PARENTAL RIGHTS

In the early twentieth century, when the U.S. Supreme Court ruled in favor of students, it did so in the context of parental rights. None of the various student cases we've discussed reached the highest court in the land—the so-called "Court of Last Resort." The Supreme Court—as the highest court in the land—has and had the power to grant student rights. But it did not do so until much later in the century.

The closest the Court came to protecting students was in two cases involving the rights of parents. The first was *Meyer v. Nebraska* (1923), a case in which the Court invalidated a Nebraska state law, passed during the jingoism of World War I, that forbade the teaching of any language other than English in any school—public or private. The law stated: "No person, individually or as a teacher, shall, in any private, denominational, parochial or public school, teach any subject to any person in any language other than the English language."

Another section of the law read: "Languages, other than the English language, may be taught as languages only after a pupil shall have attained and successfully passed the eighth grade as evidenced by a certificate of graduation issued by the county superintendent of the county in which the child resides." Officials in Hamilton

County, Nebraska, charged Robert Meyer with violating the state law for teaching German to ten-year-old Raymond Parpart at a private parochial school maintained by the Zion Evangelical Lutheran Congregation. Parpart had not graduated from the eighth grade, so Meyer was placed within the crosshairs of the law.

The Nebraska state courts upheld the law, reasoning that it was a just exercise of the state's general powers needed to ensure that immigrants were educated in English. "The salutary purpose of the statute is clear," the court wrote. "The legislature had seen the baneful effects of permitting foreigners, who had taken residence in this country, to rear and educate their children in the language of their native land. The result of that condition was found to be inimical to our own safety."

State supreme court justice Charles B. Letton dissented from his colleagues, finding that the legislation infringed upon the fundamental rights of parents. "Every parent has the fundamental right . . . to give his child such further education in proper subjects as he desires and can afford," he wrote. Letton characterized the law as an intemperate response to fears generated by the German threat in World War I: "It is patent, obvious, and a matter of common knowledge that this restriction was the result of crowd psychology; that it is a product of the passions engendered by the World War, which have had not had time to cool."

Meyer appealed to the U.S. Supreme Court, which reversed the lower court's decision. "Mere knowledge of the German language cannot reasonably be regarded as harmful," wrote Justice James C. McReynolds for the Court. The decision focused solely on the rights of the teacher and the parents, not the students. "His right thus to teach and the right of parents to engage him so to instruct their children, we think, are within the liberty of the amendment," McReynolds wrote, failing to mention anything about the rights of students.

The *Meyer* decision stands for the principle that parents have a Fourteenth Amendment liberty interest under the Due Process Clause regarding their right to rear their children as they see fit. The

Supreme Court reaffirmed this principle a few years later in *Pierce v. Society of Sisters* (1925), which examined an Oregon law that required students in the state to attend public school. Two private schools challenged the law on due process grounds.

The Supreme Court invalidated the Oregon measure, noting that it would lead to the abolition of private schools. "The inevitable practical result of enforcing the act . . . would be destruction of . . . perhaps all other private primary schools for normal children within the state of Oregon."

The Court relied on its earlier *Meyer* decision for the principle of strong parental rights. "Under the doctrine of *Meyer v. Nebraska*, we think it entirely plain that the Act of 1922 unreasonably interferes with the liberty of parents and guardians to direct the upbringing and education of children under their control," the Court wrote. "The child is not the mere creature of the state; those who nurture him and direct his destiny have the right, coupled with the high duty, to recognize and prepare him for additional obligations."

Today, parents often raise parental rights claims in cases involving student expression. For example, parents across the country claim that mandatory school uniform policies not only infringe on their children's free expression rights but also violate their parental rights to control the rearing of their children. Sometimes parents assert similar claims with respect to certain material that is taught to their children to which they object—such as information about birth control and contraceptives.

The *Meyer* and *Pierce* decisions are important to student rights for at least two reasons. First, they involved U.S. Supreme Court decisions invalidating laws that impacted or limited students' rights. Second, they showed that the courts at that time did not even consider the First Amendment in relation to student rights. Claims were evaluated under a different constitutional amendment altogether. But, the case had an impact decades later when the Supreme Court cited them for the principle that schools were not Constitution-free zones and that school officials had to respect students and their freedoms under the Bill of Rights.

TRAILBLAZERS

The stories of most of the student litigants mentioned so far are not well known. Perhaps that's because history looks more favorably on the victors than the losers. In spite of his loss, Earl Wooster, the bold young man who stood up at a school assembly and challenged officials about fire safety issues, did have a lasting impact in education and the lives of countless students.

Of course, before he could embark on his career in education, Wooster had to obtain a diploma. School officials in Fresno had withheld his diploma after his infamous speech about fire escapes and overbearing school authority.

After his failed litigation over the diploma, Wooster approached school officials. "I told them that I would like to go to the University and that I'd like to get my diploma," Wooster later recalled. "They said they had no hard feelings toward me. It never was a personal proposition; they'd be very happy to give me my diploma. One of them even offered me money to go to college on." With his diploma finally in hand, he entered the University of Nevada. Graduating from college in 1922, Wooster began working as a teacher in Fallon, Nevada. He later became a principal and school superintendent in Washoe County. As superintendent, he oversaw the hiring of the district's first African American and Native American instructors. In 1958, the Nevada State Education Association awarded Earl Wooster the Distinguished Service Award. From 1958 to 1965, he served as executive secretary of the Nevada State Educational Association. Later, the school board in Reno honored him by naming a high school Earl Wooster High School—the name it bears today. Students at the school also named the honor society after Wooster— who many years before had the temerity to challenge school officials.

PAVING THE WAY

Earl Wooster, Pearl Pugsley, and other students paved the way for future generations. These young litigants bravely took on the legal system at a time before First Amendment jurisprudence had developed and before the concept of student rights entered public consciousness. In other words, they came before their time. Their disputes came before the U.S. Supreme Court had developed First Amendment law. These students of the nineteenth and early twentieth centuries faced an environment not concerned about any free speech rights. The social and legal milieu focused on reasonable rules, judicial deference to school officials, and the duty of students to obey authority. Unless a school rule transgressed all bounds of reasonableness, a court would uphold the law and view the student lawsuits as annoyances if not with outright disdain. This was the body of law that Justice Thomas cited with approval in his concurring opinion in 2007. He wanted the Court to return to the rule of reasonableness.

But the law evolves and so does society. The Supreme Court has interpreted the First Amendment more broadly and applied it to state and local governments. In this changing environment, another group of students—largely Jehovah's Witnesses—would follow in the wake of these early student litigants and greatly advance the cause of student rights. They would start by bringing the First Amendment into the public schools.

CHAPTER 2

THE "FIXED STAR"

U.S. Supreme Court justice Harlan Fiske Stone once wrote that the "Jehovah's Witnesses ought to have an endowment in view of the aid which they give in solving the legal problems of civil liberties." First Amendment law—and more specifically student speech law—owes a large debt of gratitude to the Jehovah's Witnesses. Between 1938 and 1946, the Supreme Court handed down more than twenty opinions involving members of the besieged religious group. Most of the opinions involved adults prosecuted for distributing religious tracts on Sundays without obtaining permits from local authorities.

But two of those opinions involved First Amendment claims brought by public school students punished for refusing to salute the American flag and recite the Pledge of Allegiance. The first of the two cases—*Minersville School District v. Gobitis* (1940)—resulted in a victory for school officials and sadly unleashed a wave of persecution against the Witnesses. The second case—*West Virginia State Board of Education v. Barnette* (1943)—led to a stunning victory for student rights and the First Amendment.

The impetus for the two cases came from influential Jehovah's Witness leader Joseph F. Rutherford. The charismatic Rutherford had served as the religious group's president since 1917 and had coined the term "Jehovah's Witnesses" in 1931. A lawyer and dynamic speaker, Rutherford often urged his followers to challenge laws he viewed as suspect or unworthy of respect. Following his lead, many Witnesses refused to curtail their religious expression even in the face of official harassment, arrests, and imprisonment. They believed fervently in the message of Mark 16:15: "Go into all the world and preach the good news to all creation." The Witnesses continually ran afoul of local law enforcement officials for distributing religious literature without a permit, proselytizing door to door, and unabashedly rejecting local laws they deemed contrary to their teachings. Flag-salute laws represented a prime example of such laws. Originating in the late nineteenth century and picking up steam in the early part of the twentieth century, these laws generally required students to stand, put their hand over their heart, and recite the Pledge of Allegiance. The American Legion promoted the flag salute as a popular show of patriotism for its mission of "one hundred percent Americanism."

These forced displays of patriotism inspired the ire of Rutherford, who in 1935 railed against them because he felt that they were too similar to the dreaded "Heil Hitler" salutes in Nazi Germany. Hitler ordered the prosecution of many Witnesses for their refusal to show obedience and subservience to him. Rutherford blasted Hitler's abuses and labeled American flag-salute laws as idolatry and an example of "unfaithfulness to God." He directed his followers to the Book of Exodus (20: 3–5), which warns believers not to "make unto thee any graven image," nor to "bow down thyself to graven images."

After Rutherford's objections to flag salutes, a young boy named Carleton Nicholls Jr. refused to salute the flag at his school in Lynn, Massachusetts, in September 1935. The Lynn school required the recitation of the Pledge at least once a week. Young Carleton had given the flag salute for two years but after Rutherford's denunciation, the eight-year-old boy began standing silently during the Pledge. His father supported his son's act, saying that Carleton declined to participate "because he was being called upon to adore the flag and to bow down to the flag and that according to his religious views, he could only adore and bow down to Jehovah."

Local authorities arrested the boy's father after he went to the school to protest the flag-salute law and the treatment of his son. The Lynn school board voted unanimously to expel young Carleton from school. Nicholls sued in state court but found no relief in the Massachusetts judiciary. The salute and pledge "are directed to a justifiable end in the conduct of education in the public schools," ruled the Massachusetts Supreme Judicial Court in *Nicholls v. Lynn* (1937).

The plight of Carleton Nicholls was not unique. Richard Ellis explains in his book *To the Flag: An Unlikely History of the Pledge of Allegiance* that school officials across the country expelled Witness children at an alarming rate for refusing to respect the flag. He reports that by the fall of 1936, at least 134 children in thirteen states had been expelled. Several of them were beaten for their supposedly brazen refusal to follow direction from school officials. Rutherford seized upon these horrific incidents, urging other adherents to follow the path of Nicholls and his father.

One of those devout adherents was Walter Gobitis, a lifelong resident of the coal-mining town of Minersville, Pennsylvania, who had been reared as a Catholic. Gobitis (the real spelling of the family surname was "Gobitas" but a court clerk error changed it to "Gobitis," and this spelling is generally used in discussions of the case) became a true believer of the Jehovah's Witnesses after reading literature provided by his wife's parents. Gobitis and his wife—who had been a practicing Methodist despite her Witness upbringing— converted full force to their new faith. A popular grocer in town, Gobitis was not shy about standing up for what he believed.

Gobitis took Rutherford's message to heart and in turn preached the message to his school-age children, Lillian and William, who were in the seventh and fifth grades respectively. He taught his children the faith but did not require them to refuse to salute the flag, leaving that to each of them as a personal decision. One day fifth-grader William came home and proudly announced at dinner that he had not saluted the flag like his classmates. Lillian, who at the time was president of her seventh-grade class, followed suit.

At the time, there was no regulation prohibiting such action in the Minersville Public Schools, which greatly irritated school superintendent Charles E. Roudabush. Teachers and students saluted the flag as a matter of policy, but there was no official rule mandating it and no procedure for punishing those who might have the audacity to buck the system. The superintendent quickly and efficiently pushed for the adoption of such a rule, and the school board complied. The new rule required that students must salute the flag and recite the Pledge of Allegiance. If students failed to follow the directive, then they could be expelled for their "act of insubordination" and their parents face criminal charges.

After the rule's adoption, Roudabush declared at a school board meeting: "I hereby expel from the Minersville schools Lillian Gobitis, William Gobitis, and Edmund Wasliewski for this act of insubordination." As a result, Gobitis had to pay for his children to attend the Jones Kingdom School, a private Jehovah's Witness school in New Ringgold. The school was thirty miles away from Minersville, which imposed financial and other hardships on the Gobitis family. Gobitis eventually helped purchase a school bus and took his and other children down dirt roads for two hours every day to school. In Peter Irons's book *The Courage of Their Convictions*, Lillian Gobitis recalled the hardships her family endured: "We didn't think our ordeal was pitiful. We had a good time. But when I look back, it was pitiful."

Gobitis sued on behalf of his children in May 1937. The Witnesses' attorneys had believed that a test case should be filed in federal court, as they had lost several cases in state courts. Besides the Nicholls loss in Massachusetts, a family in New Jersey also lost in a state court.

The choice to file in federal court proved somewhat fortuitous. In an early piece of good luck, the judge hearing the case was Judge Albert B. Maris, a Quaker appointed to the bench by President Franklin D. Roosevelt. Although he was a patriotic, decorated World War I veteran and a personal supporter of flag salutes, Maris took the principle of religious freedom very seriously. In his first opinion in *Gobitis v. Minersville School District* (1937), Maris refused to dismiss the lawsuit, finding that "the refusal to salute the flag does not prejudice the public safety." Maris also evoked the memory of the founder of the state—Quaker William Penn—and his religious persecution in England. "We may well recall that William Penn, founder of Pennsylvania, was expelled from Oxford University for his refusal for conscience' sake to comply with regulations not essentially dissimilar, and suffered, more than once, imprisonment in England because of his religious convictions." Maris found that the case had merit under both the Pennsylvania and U.S. constitutions.

Maris held a hearing in February 1938. During court testimony, Lillian Gobitis recited the biblical verse 1 John 5:21: "Little children, keep yourselves from idols." The other side objected to the recital of this and other Bible verses, but Judge Maris quickly rejected the petty objections. The judge reasoned that the matter was relevant because the reason for the Witnesses' refusal to comply was their sincere religious beliefs.

Maris's handling of the court hearing gave Gobitis and his lawyers cause for optimism, as he seemed sensitive to their religious convictions. Four months later, Maris's opinion confirmed their positive impression of him as an able and fair-minded jurist. He rejected the school's argument that refusal to salute the flag somehow harmed other students and threatened the operation of the school. "I think it is also clear from the evidence that the refusal of these two earnest Christian children to salute the flag cannot even remotely prejudice or imperil the safety, health, morals, property or personal rights of their fellows," he wrote. "While I cannot agree with them I nevertheless cannot but admit that they exhibit sincerity of conviction and devotion to principle in the face of opposition of a piece with that which brought our pioneer ancestors across the sea to seek liberty of conscience in a new land."

Judge Maris ordered the Minersville School District to allow the Gobitis children back into school and to desist from forcing them to salute the flag. The school appealed to the U.S. Court of Appeals for the Third Circuit and Maris stayed his ruling pending the appeal process.

The Minersville School District did not fare better before the three-judge panel of the Third Circuit. Writing for a unanimous panel, Judge William R. Clark captured the David-versus-Goliath aspect of the case quite nicely in his opening sentence: "Eighteen big states have seen fit to exert their power over a small number of little children." He recounted the history of flag-salute laws, tracing them to an October 1892 National Public School celebration—the year that a socialist named Francis Bellamy wrote the Pledge. Clark quoted with approval a historian who referred to flag-salute laws as forms of "false patriotism." He also quoted from Laurens M. Hamilton, a descendent of Alexander Hamilton, who noted that "we must beware of legislation such as that forcing people to salute the flag."

Judge Clark then cited many sources on religion and the importance of religious liberty. He ended his opinion by quoting George Washington, who wrote that "the conscientious scruples of all men should be treated with great delicacy and tenderness." Clark said that the Minersville School Board abjectly failed to "treat 'the conscientious scruples' of all children with that 'great delicacy and tenderness.' We agree with the father of our country that they should and we concur with the learned District Court in saying that they must."

SUPREME DEFEAT

The Minersville School District pressed forward to the U.S. Supreme Court. School superintendent Roudabush considered Clark's opinion for the Third Circuit "a hodgepodge of perverted quotations." The attorney for the school district contended that reciting the Pledge was a patriotic exercise, not a religious ceremony. He emphasized the importance of the salute toward fostering love of country in young students—an essential quality in productive citizens.

The Witnesses had a "dream team" of lawyers, including their own Joseph Rutherford, Hayden Covington—who would go on to represent the Witnesses in more than forty cases before the U.S. Supreme Court—and George Gardner, a Harvard law professor who argued on behalf of the American Civil Liberties Union (ACLU). The ACLU had intervened in the case and filed an amicus—or friend-of-the-court—brief before the Court. Justice Felix Frankfurter, who had also taught at Harvard Law School, emerged as a tough questioner at oral argument—particularly of his former colleague Gardner.

The Supreme Court justices met in conference to discuss their impressions of the case. Chief Justice Charles Evans Hughes assigned what he thought would be the Court's unanimous opinion to Frankfurter, who spoke with enthusiasm on the need for patriotism and national unity, as the country entered World War II. An immigrant from Austria, Frankfurter believed that the flag salute played an important role in instilling love of country. But Frankfurter also had a civil-liberties background, having served as a leading member of the ACLU celebrated in some circles for his defense of the Italian anarchists Ferdinando Sacco and Bartolomeo Vanzetti, whom many suspected did not receive a fair trial in a murder prosecution.

Frankfurter did not disappoint the chief justice with his opinion though he noted the "conflicting claims of liberty and authority." Writing that "every possible leeway should be given to the claims of religious faith," Frankfurter still sided with the school officials and in favor of the mandatory flag-salute rule. "The ultimate foundation of a free society is the binding tie of cohesive sentiment," he wrote. "Such a sentiment is fostered by all those agencies of the mind and spirit which may serve to gather up the traditions of a people, transmit them from generation to generation, and thereby create that continuity of a treasured common life which constitutes a civilization. 'We live by symbols.' The flag is the symbol of our national unity, transcending all internal differences, however large, within the framework of the Constitution."

Frankfurter also wrote that courts should defer to the wisdom of school officials, who know best how to educate young children—a familiar refrain in early school law cases. This meant that Lillian and William Gobitis's First Amendment claims met the same fate as those of Earl Wooster, Pearl Pugsley, and countless others before them.

Justice Harlan Fiske Stone authored a solitary dissent, arguing that the school officials had violated the religious liberty and conscience of these young children. He believed that Minersville school officials could not "compel pubic affirmations which violate their religious conscience."

"It was against us, eight to one," Lillian Gobitis said years later to legal scholar Peter Irons. "Talk about a cold feeling! We absolutely did not expect that. That just set off a wave of persecution. It was like open season on Jehovah's Witnesses." Vigilantes attacked groups of Witnesses in numerous Texas towns, in what appeared to be a dangerous streak of jingoism. Reports of abuse became so rampant that Solicitor General Francis Biddle and Attorney General Robert Jackson spoke out publicly against the injustices inflicted upon Witnesses. The ACLU in its 1941 pamphlet *The Persecution of Jehovah's Witnesses* reported that 1,500 Witnesses had endured nearly 350 mobbings in forty-four states. More than 600 Witnesses were arrested in Texas alone between 1941 and 1942. In West Virginia, several Witnesses were roped like cattle by local law enforcement. One Witness in Nebraska was castrated by an angry mob. It was a violent "open season" and change needed to come quickly for the Witnesses.

A CHANGE OF HEART

The violence perpetrated against Jehovah's Witnesses was not lost on some members of the Supreme Court. Within two years after the ruling in *Gobitis*, three members of the Court—William O. Douglas, Hugo Black, and Frank Murphy—took the unusual step of publicly stating that they had been wrong. They did so in a joint dissenting opinion in the case of one of the most unsung and courageous heroes in all of American constitutional law—an African American preacher and Witness named Rosco Jones. In his 1968 *Watchtower* article "Putting Kingdom Interests First," Jones reflected: "As I look back over the forty-odd years of service to Jehovah and count the many blessings that have been mine, I have no regrets; my joy is full. And still the Kingdom interests come first."

Putting the Kingdom's interests first often placed Jones and his wife, Thelma, in great danger. Rosco and Thelma traveled around the Southeast preaching—even in all-white areas at the risk of death.

In La Grange, Georgia, Rosco narrowly survived a jailing and brutal beating from law enforcement officials. Later, he and Thelma were arrested in Opelika, Alabama, knowing that they would face the wrath of another all-white legion of law enforcement officials. That incident set the stage for the Court's decision in *Jones v. City of Opelika I* (1942), in which the majority of the Court refused to invalidate a sidewalk ordinance that punished Jones for selling religious books on a public sidewalk without a license.

In their dissenting opinion, Justices Murphy, Black, and Douglas expressed regret for the wave of violence perpetrated on Jehovah's Witnesses and for their vote in the *Gobitis* decision:

> Since we joined in the opinion in the *Gobitis* case, we think this is an appropriate occasion to state that we now believe that it also was wrongly decided. Certainly our democratic form of government, functioning under the historic Bill of Rights, has a high responsibility to accommodate itself to the religious views of minorities, however unpopular and unorthodox those views may be. The First Amendment does not put the right freely to exercise religion in a subordinate position. We fear, however, that the opinions in these and in the *Gobitis* case do exactly that.

AN AMAZING REVERSAL

The U.S. Supreme Court takes the notion of what the law calls "stare decisis" very seriously. Latin for "let the decision stand," stare decisis reflects a strong commitment to respecting past decisions or precedent. The American judicial system follows the guidance of the English common-law system where judges look to past decisions for guidance and wisdom. The Court infrequently overrules its past decisions. Almost always, such a reversal takes a very long time. In the most famous example, it took the Court fifty-eight years to overrule the noxious separate-but-equal doctrine in *Plessy v. Ferguson* (1896)—a doctrine that led to separation of the races in virtually all aspects of public life including education, recreation, lodging, and travel. The Court finally invalidated the practice of segregation in public education and the separate-but-equal doctrine in *Brown v. Board of Education* in 1954.

However, the Murphy/Black/Douglas dissent in Rosco Jones's case signaled that at least several members of the Court were eager to find a case in which they could overrule *Gobitis*. They found the vehicle to do just that in a Jehovah's Witness flag-salute case in West Virginia involving another pair of schoolchildren similar to William and Lillian Gobitis.

Gathie and Marie Barnette (like the Gobitises, they had their surname misspelled by a court clerk—as the real spelling was "Barnett") attended Slip Hill Grade School in Charleston, West Virginia. They were reared as Jehovah's Witnesses by their father, Walter, a devout Witness who worked for a local chemical company. Walter Barnette—like Walter Gobitis—followed the preachings and teachings of Joseph Rutherford. He did not believe his daughters should engage in the practice of saluting the flag. He considered it idolatry. Recalling the case sixty years later, Gathie said: "Well, they just taught us the purpose of our faith, which is to give our devotion and worship to Jehovah God, not to any image of any sort, and we were taught that the bowing down to the flag, saluting it, was like a bowing down and giving reverence to it—it was like an idol. So we believe definitely not to worship idols."

The Barnette sisters' classroom originally had a picture of the American flag on the wall. After the United States entered World War II in 1941, school officials replaced the picture with a real flag and ordered students to salute the flag and recite the Pledge of Allegiance. In January 1942, the policy became virtually statewide as the West Virginia Board of Education adopted a resolution ordering that the salute to the flag become "a regular part of the program of activities in the public schools." The state had passed a law that required school boards to teach history and civics and instill patriotism and American values in the schools. The West Virginia Board of Education followed this law by passing its rule requiring the flag salute and the recitation of the Pledge. Under the West Virginia rule refusal to salute the flag constituted insubordination, and resulted in expulsion for the offending student and jail time for the student's parents. Under the policy, parents could be prosecuted, fined, and ordered to spend up to thirty days in jail. The board of education's rule had the force of law because of the general state law requiring schools to teach American values and patriotism; in other words, the school board rule had its moorings in the overarching state law that gave authority to school boards to pass these restrictive, pro-patriotism laws. The Barnette sisters—along with students from two other families—refused to salute the flag and recite the Pledge of Allegiance. The girls' teacher noticed they were not saluting the flag and told the principal. While the Barnette sisters remember their teacher fondly, they said that the principal was less than friendly. "Our teacher was very understanding," Marie reflected in a 2009 interview. "The principal was sterner and a little less kind. He wanted to know why we wouldn't do what the other kids did."

Unsatisfied with the girls' response, the principal ordered the children home. As soon as they arrived home, the Barnette family consulted Charleston lawyer Horace Meldahl, who told the family that the sisters should still go to school in the morning and stay until the time of the flag salute. Marie explained that this was done so that local authorities would not send their father to jail for his children being delinquent or absent from school. The Barnettes sued the West Virginia State Board of Education in federal court and the case came before a panel of three judges—John J. Parker, Henry E. Watkins, and Ben Moore.

In October 1942, Judge Parker wrote a unanimous opinion in favor of the Barnettes. The opinion was unusual in the sense that Parker and his colleagues declined to follow the precedent set by the U.S. Supreme Court in Gobitis. Parker wrote that ordinarily the judges would feel the need to follow precedent, but "the developments with respect to the Gobitis case . . . are such that we do not feel that it is incumbent upon us to accept it as binding authority." Parker specifically mentioned the "special dissenting opinion" by Murphy, Black, and Douglas as a prime reason for the decision to ignore Gobitis.

Parker proceeded to write an opinion very protective of religious freedom. He noted that there had never been a "religious prosecution in history that was not justified in the eyes of those engaging in it on the ground that it was reasonable and right and that the persons whose practices were suppressed were guilty of stubborn folly hurtful to the general welfare." He further noted that the "tyranny of majorities over the rights of individuals or helpless minorities has always been recognized as one of the great dangers of popular government." He then reasoned that the flag salute had only an "indirect influence on the national safety" and could not justify such a severe intrusion on the conscience and religious freedom of these students.

The board of education appealed to the Supreme Court, where Harlan Fiske Stone now sat as chief justice, promoted by President Franklin D. Roosevelt after the retirement of Chief Justice Hughes. Stone—the lone dissenter in *Gobitis*—could have taken the majority opinion for himself but instead he assigned the task to a newer member of the Court and a real wordsmith—Robert H. Jackson, the former U.S. attorney general who had decried mob abuse against Jehovah's Witnesses. Before he joined the Court, Jackson had also authored the book entitled *The Struggle for Judicial Supremacy* (1941), in which he spoke favorably about several decisions that protected the First Amendment rights of Jehovah's Witnesses. In a footnote, Jackson then contrasted those protective decisions with *Gobitis*. Jackson wrote that "the Court has been particularly vigilant in stamping out attempts by local authorities to suppress the free dissemination of ideas, upon which the system of responsible democratic government rests."

Jackson produced one of the most important and celebrated opinions in the history of constitutional law—an opinion released on Flag Day, June 14, 1943. Distinguished law professor Charles Alan Wright wrote in 1996 that Jackson's opinion is "extraordinary . . . [in] its literary style." Jackson crafted passages that animate the essence of individual freedom in a constitutional democracy. In language that has become First Amendment lore, Jackson wrote: "If there is any fixed star in our constitutional constellation, it is that no official high or petty shall prescribe what shall be orthodox in matters of politics, nationalism, religion or other matters of opinion or force citizens to confess by word or acts their faith therein."

This passage established the compelled-speech doctrine, which holds that the government cannot compel individuals to engage in certain speech. Traditionally, the First Amendment comes into play when an individual speaks in an offensive or critical manner and the government punishes the individual. The compelled-speech doctrine recognizes that the government can also infringe on First Amendment freedoms by compelling or forcing certain messages.

Equally significant, Jackson established that public school students have First Amendment rights and that the First Amendment applies in public schools. In another oft-quoted passage, he wrote: "That they are educating the young for citizenship is reason for scrupulous protection of Constitutional freedoms of the individual, if we are not to strangle the free mind at its source and teach youth to discount important principles of our government as mere platitudes." This eloquent passage paved the way for the modern-day concept of student rights. If students don't live in an environment that respects their constitutional rights, they will grow up cynical and unappreciative of constitutional freedoms. Free speech could become a "mere platitude" instead of our first freedom. It is a lesson lost on many school officials even to this day.

Three justices dissented from Jackson's majority opinion—Felix Frankfurter, Stanley Reed, and Owen Roberts. Frankfurter wrote a passionate dissent that began on an unusually personal note that spoke to his Jewish heritage: "One who belongs to the most vilified and persecuted minority in history is not likely to be insensible to the freedoms guaranteed by our Constitution." Yet Frankfurter also felt that the Court had overstepped its bounds and intruded into the proper sphere of the legislative branch and local school officials. "We may deem [the flag salute] a foolish measure, but the point is that this Court is not the organ of government to resolve doubts as to whether it will fulfill its purpose," he wrote.

But it was Jackson's opinion that became the law of the land. It overruled *Gobitis*, causing *Time* magazine to run a story with the headline "Blot Removed." It changed First Amendment law and student rights forever. As legal commentator Stuart Leviton wrote, it established a "constitutional baseline" for students' First Amendment rights.

OTHER PLEDGE CONTROVERSIES

While the celebrated *Barnette* decision made clear that students couldn't be forced to recite the Pledge, it did not resolve or end controversies over the Pledge of Allegiance. The Pledge itself underwent a controversial change in 1954, when, in the midst of Cold War concerns, Congress added the words "under God" to emphasize the stark differences between religious Americans and "Godless Communists." That two-word addition led to legal challenges based on the first ten words of the First Amendment—the Establishment Clause.

This is the clause providing that "Congress shall make no law respecting an establishment of religion." No area of the First Amendment engenders more controversy, as people vigorously disagree over the meaning of the Establishment Clause. It clearly means that the government cannot create a national church, favor one religious sect over another, or, in the opinion of most observers, favor religion over non-religion. Several lawsuits have been filed through the years contending that the addition of the words "under God" in the Pledge amounts to the government endorsing or promoting religion in violation of the Establishment Clause.

Most famously—or infamously depending on your point of view—an emergency room physician with a law degree named Michael Newdow challenged the constitutionality of the Pledge in federal court on behalf of his elementary-school-age daughter. In 2002, a three-judge panel of the U.S. Appeals Court for the Ninth Circuit ruled in *Newdow v. United States Congress* that the forced recitation of the Pledge violated the Establishment Clause. That opinion created a maelstrom of negative reaction the likes of which had rarely been seen for lower court decisions. The U.S. Senate and House passed resolutions condemning the decision with near unanimity.

Two years later, the U.S. Supreme Court reversed the Ninth Circuit's decision in *Elk Grove Unified School District v. Newdow* (2004), reasoning that the divorced Newdow lacked standing to bring the suit because he did not have primary legal custody of his daughter. Like the 1943 *Barnette* ruling, the Court's decision was issued on Flag Day.

The controversy over the Establishment Clause and the Pledge are far from over, as Newdow—who has a website entitled "Restore Our Pledge of Allegiance"—filed another challenge on behalf of other parents with children who objected to the Pledge in their public schools. The case was still on appeal in the federal court system at the time of this writing. Whatever the ultimate outcome, any future Establishment Clause decisions on the Pledge likely will do little to move the needle on students' rights.

The needle could be moved, however, with regard to another continuing Pledge controversy. Remarkably, to this day students are still punished for refusing to salute the flag, as William Gobitis and Marie Barnette were so very many years ago. Many of these disputes involve school officials ignoring or trampling upon the compelled-speech principle of *Barnette*. After the terrorist attacks of September 11, 2001, many state legislatures passed Pledge of Allegiance laws requiring the oath's recitation. In other jurisdictions, individual students face punishment for refusing to take part in the exercise because of mandatory school rules, even without laws requiring it.

In 2000, Alabama school officials disciplined high school student Michael Holloman for raising his fist during the recitation of the Pledge of Allegiance as a measure of support for a classmate who had refused to recite the Pledge. Holloman believed that his classmate had been unfairly punished. A federal district court judge dismissed his lawsuit, but Holloman appealed. In *Holloman v. Harland* (2004), the U.S. Court of Appeals for the Eleventh Circuit reinstated his lawsuit, writing that "*Barnette* clearly and specifically established that schoolchildren have the right to refuse to say the Pledge of Allegiance." The panel concluded that "Holloman had the constitutional right to raise his fist during the Pledge of Allegiance so long as he did not disrupt the educational process or the class in any real way."

Another legal dispute occurred in Florida in 2004, where high school student Cameron Frazier arrived at his fourth-period math class and decided to sit during the Pledge of Allegiance. His math teacher berated him in front of the class. "You clearly have no respect. You are so ungrateful and so un-American," the teacher told him. "Do you know what's out there fighting our war? That flag you refuse to show respect to." Frazier fired back: "No, our soldiers are out fighting a war. The flag is an inanimate piece of cloth that doesn't move and surely can't hold a gun." Frazier was punished for violating a 1942 Florida law—passed before the *Barnette* decision—that required students to "stand at attention" during the Pledge. Another part of the law required students to obtain their parents' written permission before being excused from the Pledge. In July 2008, the Eleventh Circuit—following its decision in the Michael Holloman case—ruled in *Frazier v. Winn* that students have a constitutional right to remain seated during the Pledge. However, the panel refused to strike down the part of the law that required students to be excused only with the written request of their parents.

In January 2009, the full Eleventh Circuit declined to review the case over the strong objection of Judge Rosemary Barkett, who contended that the panel's decision "directly contravenes" *Barnette*. She wrote that "the right to exercise one's conscience in not reciting the Pledge lies solely with the individual student, not with the parents of that student and certainly not with the State." Cameron Frazier, represented by the ACLU, appealed to the U.S. Supreme Court. His petition stated that the Florida law "undermines the right of individual conscience that *Barnette* enshrined as a bedrock principle of First Amendment law." The U.S. Supreme Court declined to review Frazier's appeal in October 2009.

The controversies involving Michael Holloman, Cameron Frazier, and a handful of others show that many school officials even in the twenty-first century fail to appreciate the lessons of the Supreme Court's *Barnette* decision. These officials have lost sight of what Justice Jackson referred to as the "fixed star"—that the government can't compel students to engage in patriotic affirmations. If school officials continue to punish students for refusing to salute the flag and recite the Pledge of Allegiance, then more young people will regard the First Amendment as a "mere platitude" instead of as a vital principle of personal freedom. Lillian Gobitis, Marie Barnette, and a group of other brave Jehovah's Witnesses did not view individual freedom, religious liberty, and student rights as "mere platitudes." Their battles ushered in new possibilities for students—possibilities that grew even stronger during the time of the civil rights movement and the Vietnam War in the 1960s.

CHAPTER 3

BUTTONS AND ARMBANDS

The Supreme Court in *Barnette* established that students possess some level of First Amendment rights in public school. Justice Jackson's lofty language about a "fixed star" surely confirmed this.

However, the Court failed to articulate a test for determining when school officials violated students' free expression rights. It was one thing for the Court to say that the government couldn't compel students to engage in practices antithetical or antagonistic to their religious faith. It was different for the Court to say that students could use the schools to protest injustices in the outside world, such as the denial of voting rights, the segregation of schools, or an unpopular war in Vietnam. The Court's decision in *Barnette* created confusion as to its constitutional moorings. Questions arose about whether the Court based its decision on the First Amendment's Free Exercise Clause or Free Speech Clause, on both, or on something else. In other words, debate continued on whether the Court had ruled in favor of the Jehovah's Witnesses because it felt school officials had infringed on their ability to freely practice their religious faith (free exercise) or because the officials had violated their free speech rights.

The uncertainties of *Barnette* meant that school officials and students did not know the precise contours of First Amendment rights in schools. In many schools, students still possessed few rights of free expression. It was not until more than twenty-five years later that the U.S. Supreme Court would articulate a legal standard for student First Amendment rights—a test for future generations of students and school officials to follow and observe. That standard arose out of the civil rights movement—a movement in which young people often stood on the front lines, some even risking their lives in the process.

Why did it take so long for the Court to establish a clear test for student First Amendment rights? Part of the reason was that the bulk of student First Amendment challenges in the 1940s, 1950s, and 1960s focused on the thorny problem of religion in schools. Just as the Establishment Clause—"Congress shall make no law respecting an establishment of religion"—represents the first ten words of the First Amendment, it also represented the vanguard of Supreme Court First Amendment jurisprudence. The Establishment Clause clearly requires a degree of separation between church and state, but the country disagrees mightily over exactly how much separation is required.

Around the time World War II was ending, groups of students and parents began challenging the practice in public schools of teachers leading students in prayer. Parents contended that prayers led by school officials placed just as much coercive pressure upon religious minorities as the forced flag salutes prohibited by *Barnette*.

Student litigants sometimes prevailed and sometimes lost in lower courts across the country. Whenever courts disagree, the likelihood of Supreme Court review increases. Fortunately for the challengers, the claim that their religious freedom had been violated would find a friendlier forum at the U.S. Supreme Court after President Dwight D. Eisenhower appointed a moderate Republican named Earl Warren as chief justice in October 1953.

While governor of California, Warren had supported the internment of Japanese Americans during World War II, a political position widely considered to be a signal of his conservative, authoritarian values. Once appointed to the Supreme Court, Warren surprised many with a seemingly progressive commitment to constitutional freedoms. One of those he surprised the most was President Eisenhower, who later referred to Warren and another appointee, William Brennan—who later became a leading liberal on the Court—as big "mistakes." The Warren Court ushered in a new era that many legal scholars termed a constitutional revolution.

FIGHTS IN SCHOOLS

In 1958, the New York Board of Regents adopted a nondenominational twenty-two-word prayer that it "recommended" be adopted in various school districts in the state. The families of five New York students, including Steven Engel, considered the mandatory, one-size-fits-all prayer intrusive, offensive, and overbearing. Though Engel was himself a religious Jew, he considered religion a personal matter, to be practiced in the home, not in the public schools. The U.S. Supreme Court ruled 6–1 (two justices did not participate in the case) in favor of Engel and his co-plaintiffs in 1962. The ruling prohibited school officials from leading students in prayer.

Justice Hugo Black wrote the Court's majority opinion, focusing on the religious persecution that forced many colonists to seek refuge in North America in the first place. "It is a matter of history that this very practice of establishing governmentally composed prayers for religious services was one of the reasons which caused many of our early colonists to leave England and seek religious freedom in America," he wrote. In his opinion, Black frequently cited founding father James Madison. For example, the Board of Regents had argued that it was a far cry from religious persecution to a simple, nondenominational prayer in public schools. In response Black quoted from Madison's famous "Memorial and Remonstrance against Religious Assessments," saying,

> To those who may subscribe to the view that because the Regents' official prayer is so brief and general there can be no danger to religious freedom in its governmental establishment, however, it may be appropriate to say in the words of James Madison, the author of the First Amendment:

"It is proper to take alarm at the first experiment on our liberties. . . . Who does not see that the same authority which can establish Christianity, in exclusion of all other Religions, may establish with the same ease any particular sect of Christians, in exclusion of all other Sects? That the same authority which can force a citizen to contribute three pence only of his property for the support of any one establishment, may force him to conform to any other establishment in all cases whatsoever?"

The next year, 1963, the Supreme Court heard a pair of cases from the states of Pennsylvania and Maryland. A Pennsylvania law required that public school students begin each day by reading ten verses from the Bible. A similar law in Maryland required officials to read either a chapter from the Bible or the Lord's Prayer at the beginning of the school day.

In the Pennsylvania case, the Schempps—a family of the Unitarian faith—challenged the law, while in the Maryland case Madalyn Murray (later known as Madalyn Murray O'Hair) disputed the law on behalf of her young son, William. School officials in both states argued that these laws served secular purposes, such as the "promotion of moral values, the contradiction to the materialistic trends of our times, the perpetuation of our institutions and the teaching of literature." Despite such arguments, the Court determined that the real purpose of the laws was an explicitly religious one—to engage in religious exercises with the Bible.

Pennsylvania and Maryland school officials had emphasized that the reading of Bible verses did not amount to the government establishing religion. The Supreme Court rejected that line of reasoning: "Further, it is no defense to urge that the religious practices here may be relatively minor encroachments on the First Amendment. The breach of neutrality that is today a trickling stream may all too soon become a raging torrent."

The Supreme Court made clear in its opinion that government officials should remain neutral toward religion rather than promoting a particular religious faith or religion in general. The Court in

Abington School District v. Schempp (1963) added that schools didn't have to become religion-free zones where the Bible could never be mentioned in the classroom. Rather, Justice Tom Clark noted that "the Bible is worthy of study for its literary and historic qualities" and "nothing we have said here indicates that such study of the Bible or of religion, when presented objectively as part of a secular program of education, may not be effected consistently with the First Amendment."

While these cases involved the Establishment Clause, a different First Amendment area than freedom of speech, they showed that the Court considered student (and parent) claims against practices in public schools as legitimate areas of inquiry. The fact that the U.S. Supreme Court would rule the day-to-day practices of school officials unconstitutional signified the dawning of a new day for the First Amendment and student rights. If the Warren Court would examine religious liberty issues in public schools, the Court could also examine free speech issues. The Court simply needed an intriguing case with disputed legal issues. The 1960s provided the perfect legal controversies in a time of mass protests over civil rights and the Vietnam War.

FREEDOM BUTTONS

In the South during the 1950s and 1960s, young people—many of them African American students—organized against the racial injustices that pervaded their daily lives. They marched, picketed, and protested. They engaged in sit-ins and other effective forms of nonviolent, direct resistance to unjust laws. As a result of their bold action, many influential civil rights cases involving First Amendment freedoms reached the Supreme Court, including *Edwards v. South Carolina* (1963).

In the *Edwards* decision, the Court invalidated the convictions of 187 protesters—many of them high school students—who marched on the South Carolina statehouse with signs bearing the message "Down with Segregation" and singing songs such as "My Country 'Tis of Thee." The protesters, who organized at Mount Zion

Baptist Church in Columbia, marched in groups of fifteen to the statehouse, where the General Assembly was in session. There, police officers arrested them for disorderly conduct. The warrants issued against the protesters charged that they breached the peace by failing to disperse from the state capitol grounds in March 1961, and that their disruptive actions "tended directly to immediate violence and breach of the peace in view of existing conditions." Some of the students received a $10 fine, while others spent as many as five days in jail.

A local magistrate convicted the students of breaching the peace, a ruling upheld by the South Carolina Supreme Court. The state high court noted that the peaceful protest had attracted the attention of a crowd of several hundred and that several adjacent streets became filled with enough people to impede traffic. The state high court characterized the arresting officers' actions as merely an attempt to maintain order and prevent any disruptions from occurring. The police officers gave the students fifteen minutes to heed their "reasonable" requests to disperse, the state high court said. Instead of leaving, the students listened to a fiery religious speech and engaged in what the city manager said was "boisterous" and "flamboyant" conduct. The state high court concurred that the acts of the students "clearly constituted a breach of the peace."

The U.S. Supreme Court read the record very differently. "The circumstances in this case reflect an exercise of these basic constitutional rights in their most pristine and classic form," wrote the Court. It noted the orderly nature of the students' protest, even quoting testimony from the police chief that there were no disruptions at the march. The Court emphasized that the Constitution "does not permit a State to make criminal the peaceful expression of unpopular views."

Similar political protests were occurring all over the country, including within the town of Philadelphia, Mississippi. There, members of various civil rights organizations and student volunteers participated in Freedom Summer, seeking to register more African Americans to vote and to protest unfair policies. Tragedy followed when three young protestors—a twenty-one-year-old African American from Meridian, Mississippi, named James Chaney and two Jewish youths from New York, Andrew Goodman and Michael Schwerner, also in their twenties—disappeared. They were believed to have been murdered in June 1964, although their bodies were not found until August. The case of the three missing civil rights workers drew national attention and forced President Lyndon Johnson to send the FBI to investigate and prosecute many local government officials, including members of law enforcement alleged to have turned the three young volunteers over to a local Ku Klux Klan chapter.

The Philadelphia murders remain a horror in American history. Though pieces of what happened that summer will never be fully known, the tragic deaths of those three crusading young people sparked very visible change.

It was against this backdrop of roiling upheaval in Mississippi that many young people, including high school students, became energized after meeting with civil rights volunteers in 1964. That year, the Council of Federated Organizations (COFO) sponsored a program that trained civil rights workers and recruited many young people to the cause. There were several sponsoring organizations in COFO including the Congress of Racial Equality (CORE), the Student Nonviolent Coordinating Committee (SNCC), and the National Association for the Advancement of Colored People (NAACP). COFO had helped form a freedom house that provided a home base and place of protection for civil rights workers. Volunteers at the Freedom House had recruited some students to circulate petitions and wear "Freedom Now" buttons.

In September 1964—one month after the three bodies of the civil rights martyrs were found—several high school students at the all-black Booker T. Washington High School in Philadelphia, Mississippi, began wearing "Freedom Now" buttons featuring the slogan "One Man, One Vote" with the acronym SNCC inscribed in the center of the buttons. Students at the high school regularly wore other types of buttons to school, including those in support of a popular new band called the Beatles. But Principal Montgomery Moore, himself African American, objected to the freedom buttons, believing that they "didn't have any bearing on [the students'] education" and "would cause commotion."

Professor Kristi Bowman explains in a 2009 law review article that Principal Moore's reaction was understandable given the context of the times: "The White community likely would have reacted with hostility at best and violence visited upon the principal and his family at worst. The state of Mississippi still funded White supremacist organizations, and clearly law enforcement in the Philadelphia area was no friend to African-Americans."

Defiantly, dozens of children still wore their freedom buttons, prompting Moore to call some thirty or forty students into his office and explain to them the importance of discipline. He offered the students the choice of removing the buttons and returning to class or going home. Many students went home. Moore then suspended the uncooperative students for a week and sent a letter to their parents. The letter read:

> Dear Parent:
> This is to inform you that your child has been suspended from school until you can come and have a talk with me. It is against school policy for anything to be brought into the school that is not educational.

Two parents—Margaret Burnside and Ola B. Morris—objected to Moore's punishment and filed suit in federal district court on behalf of their children. Burnside sued on behalf of her children, Canzater and Martha. Morris sued on behalf of her child, Ajatha. Later a third woman, Mrs. English, joined the suit on behalf of her young daughter, Neva. The suit alleged numerous constitutional violations, including the claim that the suppression of the freedom buttons violated the students' core First Amendment rights. The students sought an injunction to prohibit school officials from enforcing the button ban and taking further disciplinary action against them.

The students were represented by an amazing group of lawyers that included Henry Aronson, who worked for the NAACP's Legal Defense Fund in Mississippi. Aronson, who was white and Jewish, had previously worked as a staff attorney for Aetna Life Insurance in Hartford, Connecticut, after graduating from Yale Law School. While enjoying the comfortable life of a corporate attorney, the twenty-nine-year-old Aronson received a phone call from former classmate Alan Levine urging him to serve as a civil rights attorney on a volunteer basis for a time in the South. Levine informed his friend that he was working with the Summer Project in Mississippi as part of the Lawyers' Constitutional Defense Committee (LCDC).

Aronson applied for and received some time off from Aetna to go to the South. However, the LCDC had enough volunteer attorneys in Mississippi so they placed Aronson in Alabama. His first job was to provide legal assistance to several hundred protesters in Selma. As Tom Cohen writes in his book *Three Who Dared*: "Perhaps for the first time in his life, [Aronson] found himself deeply interested in somebody other than Henry Aronson."

In Selma, Aronson saw up close and personal a world completely unfamiliar to him. "Jim Clarke, the sheriff in Selma, beat the living shit out of me," he recalled. "That was the moment in which I knew I had to become more involved in the fight for civil rights and justice."

After his work in Alabama, Aronson never returned to insurance law but went to Mississippi to work for the NAACP's Legal Defense Fund. Aronson and others, including another Yale Law graduate, Marian Wright, who would later become one of the most prominent African American activists in the nation, performed legal work for civil rights volunteers, protestors, and organizers. "Philadelphia was a very scary place at that time," Aronson recalled. "But these kids were the feistiest kids, they had amazing strength and courage to do what they did at that time and under those circumstances. In their community three people had just been murdered and there was violent enforcement of Jim Crow laws."

Aronson also credited the three mothers—Burnside, English, and Morris—for suing on their daughters' behalf. "Their strength was in allowing their kids to sue in the first place," he explained. "You have to understand that in that day and age bombings were endemic, beatings were endemic, and firings were endemic. When people protested and sued, they were in jeopardy for their property, jobs, and even lives."

While Aronson has positive recollections of the young students and their parents, he does not harbor the same feelings for the presiding judge in the matter—U.S. district judge Sidney Mize. "In the Southern District of Mississippi at that time there were two federal district court judges—Harold Cox and Sidney Mize. Cox was a virulent racist, just a dreadful man," Aronson said. "He actually used the word *nigger* in court."Aronson said that Mize was different. "He was a passive segregationist, awful in his rulings but far more genteel than Cox." During a hearing in Mize's courtroom, Aronson elicited powerful testimony from fourteen-year-old Neva English, identified in the opinion only as "Miss English."

ARONSON:	What were you trying to do with those buttons?
ENGLISH:	Our rights to speech and to do [the] things we would like to do.
ARONSON:	What kind of things would you like to do?
ENGLISH:	Go uptown and sit in the drugstores and wherever we buy things uptown we can sit down and won't have to walk right out at the time we get it.
ARONSON:	What else?
ENGLISH:	And to register and vote without being beat up and killed.

Despite this powerful testimony, Mize denied the students' claims in an oral ruling from the bench. He determined that the ban on buttons was "reasonably necessary to maintain proper discipline in the school." It was no great surprise that Mize ruled against the plaintiffs in this civil rights case. A few years earlier he had ruled against James Meredith, who sued after being denied admission to the University of Mississippi (Ole Miss). Mize had reluctantly reprimanded the state's assistant attorney general, who argued for the university, for referring repeatedly to Meredith in court as a "nigra." The U.S. Court of Appeals for the Fifth Circuit had reversed Mize's decision then, and the litigants in the Philadelphia, Mississippi, school case hoped the Fifth Circuit would do the same for them. They got their wish, unlike their counterparts in another part of the state.

A story similar to the one unfolding at Booker T. Washington High School began playing out in Rolling Forks, Mississippi, at Henry Weathers High School in January 1965, when thirty students wore freedom buttons to class. The principal, O. E. Jordan, ordered the students to remove the buttons. The next Monday, about 150 students came to class wearing buttons. They fervently believed that they had the right to protest the injustices they saw on a daily basis. The following day—February 2—nearly 200 students wore the freedom buttons in the school gymnasium. The principal reiterated that if the students came to school the next day with the buttons, they would face a suspension.

On February 3, many students defiantly returned to school with their buttons. The principal ordered them home and suspended. But one student went into class anyway and started a disturbance. A school bus driver walked into another classroom and began distributing even more buttons. Principal Jordan had had enough—he ordered many students suspended for the rest of the year. More than 300 students were suspended from various schools in the district.

The NAACP filed suit on behalf of the suspended students in *Blackwell v. Issaquena County Board of Education,* contending that they should be readmitted to school and that the punishment violated their First Amendment rights to engage in political speech. The district court refused to grant them an injunction and ruled in favor of the school officials. The NAACP appealed to the Fifth Circuit. That court was fast becoming a crucial battleground for student speech and civil rights litigation.

A LEGAL PRECEDENT

For many years in this country, the judicial system offered little hope or justice to dispossessed or aggrieved minorities. Courts often were openly hostile to individual rights claims, particularly if they came from African Americans. A beacon of hope developed in the South in the form of several federal jurists on the U.S. Fifth Circuit. Great jurists such as Elbert Tuttle, John Minor Wisdom, and J. Skelly Wright reviewed decisions in discrimination cases by federal trial court judges and sometimes reversed those decisions. Author Jack Bass called them "Unlikely Heroes" in his book by that name, detailing how the Fifth Circuit judges dismantled segregation through a series of rulings in the 1960s and 1970s. One of these "unlikely heroes" was Walter Pettus Gewin from Alabama, a former president of the Alabama Bar Association. Gewin identified with the pioneering spirit of those students in the *Burnside* case who peacefully wore freedom buttons without disrupting school activities. Gewin was one of three judges who heard both of the freedom button cases, *Burnside* and *Blackwell*.

In arguments before the Fifth Circuit panel, attorneys for the students made several arguments. They argued that the school officials were not justified in suppressing the students' political speech. They contended that students in public schools had the same free speech rights as adult citizens—a result the Fifth Circuit would not likely adopt. However, Aronson also put forth another legal argument—one that would leave a lasting legacy in the struggle for student First Amendment rights. He argued that the students in the *Burnside* case should be protected because they did not cause a disruption. "I came to that legal position intuitively and also with help from Anthony Amsterdam, who was the brains of the [NAACP's] Legal Defense Fund," Aronson said. "We knew there had to be some deference paid to the maintenance of order in the educational environment. So we tried to come up with a position or argument that balanced First Amendment rights with order in the schools." The result was the substantial disruption test.

The school lawyers argued for a most strident position—that students really had no free speech rights in school and that the school rules in question should be evaluated under the familiar reasonableness standard that had felled the challenges of Earl Wooster, Pearl Pugsley, and other student litigants through the years.

The Fifth Circuit adopted a position somewhere in between these opposing views: the students' contention that wearing the buttons posed no clear and present danger to order in the school and the school officials' position that students had no First Amendment rights at all. The Fifth Circuit adopted the substantial disruption test that Aronson had proposed. On July 21, 1966, the three-judge panel of the Fifth Circuit issued rulings in *Burnside v. Byars* and *Blackwell v. Issaquena County Board of Education.* Writing for the court in both opinions, Judge Gewin ruled for the students in *Burnside* but against the students in *Blackwell.* The difference—according to Gewin— came down to the level of disruption that the buttons caused at the respective high schools.

In *Burnside*, Gewin wrote that there was "only a showing of mild curiosity on the part of the other school children over the presence of some 30 or 40 other children wearing such insignia." However, in *Blackwell* Gewin wrote that the wearing of the buttons "created a state of confusion, disrupted class instruction, and resulted in a general breakdown of orderly discipline."

In his opinion in *Burnside*, Gewin noted that high school students must learn to obey school officials because "obedience . . . is a valuable tool and respect for those in authority must be instilled in our young people." However, Gewin wrote, "we must also emphasize that school officials cannot ignore expressions of feelings with which they do not wish to contend." He then crafted a passage that still bears great significance for student speech cases today:

> They [school officials] cannot infringe on their students' right to free and unrestricted expression as guaranteed to them under the First Amendment to the Constitution, where the exercise of such rights in the school buildings and schoolrooms do not materially and substantially interfere with the requirements of appropriate discipline in the operation of the school.

Blackwell presented a different story than *Burnside* because school officials presented evidence of disruption at the school. "The facts demonstrate that during the time students wore freedom buttons to school, much disturbance was created by these students," Gewin wrote in *Blackwell.* "Their actions in the school building are indeed reprehensible and the school officials certainly have the authority to mete out punishment as they deem appropriate for their discourteous behavior toward school officials."

This material and substantial interference test would prove vitally important in another student protest case—one that involved armbands rather than buttons. This case—unlike the Mississippi cases—would go all the way to the U.S. Supreme Court.

BLACK PEACE ARMBANDS

In 1965, the growing conflict in Vietnam dominated discussions from the Pentagon to the dinner tables of average Americans. Nearly 200,000 U.S. troops were stationed in Vietnam by the end of 1965 and American casualties were beginning to mount. So was opposition to American involvement and support for a truce.

In November 1965, antiwar groups marched in Washington, D.C., to protest American soldiers dying in Southeast Asia for a war that seemed remote from the problems of everyday America. Senator Robert F. Kennedy, the brother of former president John F. Kennedy and a likely presidential candidate in the next election, became a strong proponent of a so-called Christmas truce to allow for peace negotiations in Vietnam.

Attending the Washington, D.C., protest were Christopher Eckhardt and John Tinker, teenagers from Des Moines, Iowa. Eckhardt, the son of Dr. William Eckhardt and Margaret Eckhardt, attended Theodore Roosevelt High School. Tinker, the son of Leonard and Lorena Tinker, attended North High School.

The Eckhardts and the Tinkers were politically conscious. Leonard Tinker, a Methodist minister, had been removed from his church because he protested against racial discrimination. He had worked for the American Friends Service Committee, a pacifist organization, since the early 1960s. In a 2009 article for the *American University Law Review*, John's sister, Mary Beth Tinker, explained that her "parents considered themselves part of a 'Social Gospel.'" Her family was honored in 1963 by the Iowa NAACP for its activism. Margaret Eckhardt was the president of the Des Moines chapter of the Women's International League for Peace and Freedom. Many of the Iowa contingent returned from the Washington, D.C., protest energized and invigorated. They wanted to do their part back home to advocate for Kennedy's Christmas truce and protest the Vietnam conflict. They decided to meet at the Eckhardt home on December 11, 1965.

According to author and legal historian John Johnson, in his book *The Struggle for Student Rights*, Margaret Eckhardt recalled about twenty-five to thirty people attending the meeting, which included adults and college and high school students. Among those in attendance were the Tinkers.

Someone in the group suggested the idea of students wearing black armbands to school, saying they would be an ideal vehicle to mourn the casualties in Vietnam, support the Christmas truce and oppose the Vietnam War. Ross Peterson, Christopher Eckhardt's classmate, wrote an article for Roosevelt High School's student newspaper that discussed protesting the war. The article began: "Some students who are interested in expressing their grief over the deaths of soldiers and civilians in Vietnam will fast on Thursday, December 16. They will also wear black arm bands starting on that same day."

Peterson's journalism teacher and student newspaper advisor suggested that Ross talk about the article with a school administrator prior to publication. The official put Peterson on notice that the article would not be published. Word had spread around the school district that the armband protest was a live issue. The superintendent of the Des Moines schools called a meeting of local school principals and they collectively issued a ban on black armbands.

It was interesting that the school officials singled out black armbands for prohibition. Students regularly wore political campaign buttons and even Iron Crosses—a symbol associated with the German military. But the black armbands touched a raw nerve for school officials for unknown reasons and they responded with alacrity.

Eckhardt, John Tinker, his sister Mary Beth, and others decided to proceed with wearing the armbands even though they knew it violated the hastily enacted school policy. Eckhardt wore his armband to Theodore Roosevelt High School, though he did not go directly to class. Instead he walked straight to the principal's office to turn himself in for discipline. While he sat outside the principal's office for about forty-five minutes, several students taunted him. A vice principal came and spoke with Eckhardt, asking him to remove the armband. Eckhardt politely refused, asserting his constitutional rights. He was suspended.

Mary Beth Tinker, then thirteen years old, wore her armband to Warren Harding Junior High School. She proceeded directly to class without incident for much of the day. Her armband attracted no attention—even in the cafeteria—until her math teacher objected to it. He ordered Mary Beth to go to the administrative offices. There, school officials talked with her about responsibility and obeying school rules. Mary Beth politely asserted her First Amendment rights. She too earned a suspension.

Sixteen-year-old John Tinker went to North High School with his black armband. In his morning classes, he met little resistance or even comment, though later in the day a few students bothered him during gym class. Later the principal met with John and his father, Leonard. He informed the Tinkers that John was suspended but that he could return to school as long as he did not wear an armband. Two younger siblings in the Tinker family—Hope and Paul—also wore black armbands to Des Moines's James Madison Elementary School. Elementary school officials did not suspend the students but used it as a teaching moment to discuss patriotism and the Bill of Rights—a concept that apparently eluded officials at the middle and high schools.

In all, five students were suspended from Des Moines middle or high schools—Eckhardt, John and Mary Beth Tinker, Christine Singer, and Bruce Clark. The students challenged the suspensions before the school board to no avail. They also endured harassment outside of school. Vandals threw red paint on the Tinkers' house. The unknown individuals apparently chose red because that color was long associated with communism. The Tinker family also received a threatening letter on Christmas Eve and postcards with hammers and sickles, saying "Go back to Russia" or "Go back to China." Christopher Eckhardt recalled being taunted as "peace boy" by kids playing football. "I remember the red paint, the death threats coming by telephone," John Tinker said in 2009. "A radio talk-show host offered to lend a weapon to anyone who would shoot my father. There was a brick thrown through the windshield of our Volkswagen."

"I personally wasn't really terrified though sometimes I wonder why," John Tinker said more than forty years later. "I think it has to do with the fact that my parents had gone to Mississippi during the Freedom Summer events where civil rights workers were killed. So I was aware of those things. I do remember lying in my bed one night and thinking 'what if a grenade or homemade bomb is thrown through the window?' Honestly, it seemed somewhat normal compared to what other people were experiencing during the time of the civil rights movement."

The school board voted 5–2 to uphold the armband ban. The Iowa Civil Liberties Union under the direction of Craig Sawyer and another young Iowa attorney named Dan Johnston led the charge. Sawyer handled much of the battle with the school board, but Johnston became the lead attorney when the case proceeded into the court system. After losing administratively, the students represented by Johnston filed suit in federal district court. The student plaintiffs asked for an injunction to prohibit school officials from enforcing the no-armband rule. Johnston emphasized the right of the students to engage in peaceful, nondisruptive political speech or political protest.

The case proceeded to trial in July 1966 before federal district court judge Roy L. Stephenson, a decorated former U.S. Army officer appointed to the bench by President Dwight D. Eisenhower.

Johnston called to the witness stand all three of the student plaintiffs: John Tinker, Mary Beth Tinker, and Christopher Eckhardt. John Tinker testified as to the importance of wearing armbands: "When people are getting killed, it's important to me."

In September 1966, Stephenson issued his opinion in *Tinker v. Des Moines Independent Community School District*. "Officials of the defendant school district have the responsibility for maintaining a scholarly, disciplined atmosphere within the classroom," he wrote. "These officials not only have a right, they have an obligation to prevent anything which might be disruptive of such an atmosphere. Unless the actions of school officials in this connection are unreasonable, the Courts should not interfere."

Stephenson then emphasized certain controversial events surrounding the Vietnam War, including a large antiwar protest in Washington, D.C., and draft card burnings in certain areas of the country.

"While the arm bands themselves may not be disruptive, the reactions and comments from other students as a result of the arm bands would be likely to disturb the disciplined atmosphere required for any classroom," Stephenson wrote. "It was not unreasonable in this instance for school officials to anticipate that the wearing of arm bands would create some type of classroom disturbance."

The students can wear their armbands off school grounds and students can still talk about the Vietnam conflict in an "orderly manner," Stephenson reasoned. Johnston had drawn Stephenson's attention to the recent decisions of the Fifth Circuit in *Burnside* and *Blackwell*, where the appeals court had explained that school officials could punish student speech only if it created a substantial or material interference with school activities. Noting that those decisions were not binding on his court since he fell within the Eighth Circuit, Stephenson explained: "After due consideration, it is the view of the Court that actions of school officials in this realm should not be limited to those instances where there is a material or substantial interference with school discipline. School officials must be given wide discretion and if, under the circumstances, a disturbance in school discipline is reasonably to be anticipated, actions which are reasonably calculated to prevent such a disruption must be upheld by the Court." In other words, Stephenson emphasized that school officials need not wait for a disruption or interference; all they needed was a reasonable forecast of disruption.

"I thought it was an easy case and that we would win a long time before that in the federal district court," Johnston said. "The school board in my opinion did not have sufficient justification to suspend the students." John Tinker also thought they would win the case. "It was disappointing. I thought we were going to win because the principle was so clear. Other students had worn other symbols. It was what we call now viewpoint discrimination. Even as a kid I understood the principle because I had grown up in the American school system. We believed in freedom."

The students appealed Stephenson's decision to the Eighth Circuit. The attorneys initially argued the case before a panel of three appeals court judges—the normal practice in federal courts at this level. However, the Eighth Circuit then ordered that the attorneys reargue the case before the entire body of active Eighth Circuit judges—a practice known as en banc (full panel) review. On November 3, 1967, the Eighth Circuit issued a one-paragraph opinion indicating that the en banc court had split 4–4 on the question, meaning that Judge Stephenson's ruling stood.

This constituted another victory for the school board attorneys, who had now prevailed before both a federal district court and a federal court of appeals. That left only the U.S. Supreme Court for the student plaintiffs.

THE COURT OF LAST RESORT
Christopher Eckhardt traveled to Washington, D.C., to attend oral arguments in the case. It was a long and unexpected journey, Eckhardt reflected in 1999. "I knew at the time that the U.S. Supreme Court consisted of nine dudes in black robes who made decisions that affected the rest of the country," Eckhardt said. "But never in my wildest dreams did I ever think we would end up in front of the

Supreme Court." Sadly, John Tinker missed his flight and couldn't make the trip. "No, I could only get a ticket for a late flight," he recalled. "I fell asleep in the lobby, and when I woke up, the plane had already gone. It was a small airport, and I could hardly believe it. The next morning I tried to fly standby but then got bumped off of a flight in Chicago."

In oral arguments, school board attorney Allan Herrick was bombarded with an incisive line of questioning by Justice Thurgood Marshall, the former NAACP lawyer who had himself argued twenty-nine cases before the high court before President Johnson made him the country's first African American Supreme Court justice in 1967. Marshall questioned the school's position that the wearing of the armbands caused a real disruption in the schools. He asked how many students wore armbands and Herrick had to reply, "Seven." Marshall then asked in his powerful voice: "Seven out of eighteen thousand, and the school board was afraid that seven students wearing armbands would disrupt eighteen thousand. Am I correct?"

After attending oral arguments before the high court in 1968, Eckhardt thought that a majority of the justices would side with him and the Tinkers. "When I heard Justice Thurgood Marshall ask the question—'seven out of eighteen thousand, and the school board was afraid that seven students wearing armbands would disrupt eighteen thousand. Am I correct?'—then I was confident we would prevail."

Eckhardt's assessment proved correct. On February 24, 1969, the U.S. Supreme Court issued its momentous decision in *Tinker v. Des Moines Independent Community School District* in favor of the students. Justice Abe Fortas authored the Court's majority decision, which emphasized the importance of the First Amendment in public schools. In oft-cited language, he noted that "it can hardly be argued that either students or teachers shed their constitutional rights to freedom of speech or expression at the schoolhouse gate." Fortas quoted at length from Justice Jackson's famous opinion in *West Virginia State Board of Education v. Barnette*. That opening salvo in Fortas's opinion dispelled any hopes by the Des Moines school board attorneys for a Court ruling that students had no First Amendment rights at school.

Fortas then characterized the wearing of the black armbands as "akin to pure speech" and "a silent, passive expression of opinion, unaccompanied by any disorder or disturbance." That characterization spelled doom for the lower federal court victories by the school board. Fortas adopted the "substantial disruption" test from the Fifth Circuit in *Burnside v. Byars*, writing that school officials can punish student expression only when they can show a reasonable forecast of substantial disruption.

Fortas also noted that the Des Moines school officials singled out the black armbands while allowing political campaign buttons and Iron Crosses. "Clearly the prohibition of expression of one particular opinion, at least without evidence that it is necessary to avoid material and substantial interference with schoolwork or discipline, is not constitutionally permissible." Fortas again cited *Burnside v. Byars*, including Judge Gewin by name for the principle that school officials cannot suppress "expressions of feelings with which they do not wish to contend."

Other parts of the opinion read like a paean to student expression and a strong condemnation of authoritarian school control: "Undifferentiated fear or apprehension of disturbance is not enough to overcome the right to freedom of expression. . . . In our system, state-operated schools may not be enclaves of totalitarianism. . . . Students may not be regarded as closed-circuit recipients of only that which the State chooses to communicate."

Fortas articulated what came to be known as the "reasonable forecast of substantial disruption test," acknowledging that schools do not have to wait for an actual riot before censoring student expression. "As we have discussed, the record does not demonstrate any facts which might reasonably have led school authorities to forecast substantial disruption of or material interference with school activities, and no disturbances or disorders on the school premises in fact occurred." The majority believed that school officials had acted more out of "undifferentiated fear" than any type of "reasonable forecast."

AN ANGRY DISSENT

Justice Hugo Black was one of the most stalwart defenders of the First Amendment during his long tenure on the Supreme Court, which began in 1938. Together with Justice William O. Douglas, he dissented in many of the McCarthy-era decisions involving Communist defendants in the 1940s and 1950s. A former member of the Ku Klux Klan in his native state of Alabama for political purposes, Black had risen to become a respected Supreme Court justice known for his literal defense of the First Amendment—"No law means no law," he would say on occasion.

But Hugo Black worried about the rampant protests occurring across the country on college campuses. He feared that disorder and chaos were triumphing over law and order. He viewed the public schools as a place to ensure a safe learning environment free from the disruptive, chaotic influences afflicting many higher-education campuses across the country.

Consequently, he viewed the *Tinker* case very differently than Abe Fortas. Generally, when justices pen their dissenting opinions, they end them with the phrase "I respectfully dissent." In his *Tinker* dissent, Black left out the word "respectfully"; he was not happy about this majority decision.

Black emphasized the leftist leanings of the students' parents, writing that Leonard Tinker had a salary paid by the American Friends Service Committee and Christopher Eckhardt's mother was an official in the Women's International League for Peace and Freedom.

Black also scoured the record in the case to find what he considered evidence of disruption. He noted that other students made comments to the armband wearers, an older football player warned Eckhardt about wearing the armbands, and that Mary Beth Tinker's armband had disrupted her mathematics class. Black conveniently left out the fact that it was the math teacher, not Mary Beth, who decided to devote the class period to a discussion of her symbolic speech. "I think the record overwhelmingly shows that the armbands did exactly what the elected school officials and principals foresaw they would, that is, took the students' minds off their classwork and diverted them to thoughts about the highly emotional subject of the Vietnam war," Black wrote.

Black then issued a diatribe against the lawlessness he saw in many of the nation's youth. "Uncontrolled and uncontrollable liberty is an enemy to domestic peace," he wrote. "We cannot close our eyes to the fact that some of the country's greatest problems are crimes committed by the youth, too many of school age." He then squarely took aim at many students involved in civil rights protests, proclaiming that "groups of students all over the land are already running loose, conducting break-ins, sit-ins, lie-ins, and smash-ins."

Black feared that a decision in favor of the Tinkers and Christopher Eckhardt would encourage other children to flout school authority and file lawsuits challenging the system. The Court's opinion "is the beginning of a new revolutionary era of permissiveness in this country fostered by the judiciary." Black was convinced that the decision would lead to more lawsuits and contribute to the breakdown of discipline in the schools.

When asked in 1999 about Black's warning of a "revolutionary era of permissiveness," Eckhardt replied: "Thank God it is more permissive—what is America if we don't have freedom?"

Tinker changed the law for the better for countless students. The highest court in the land had ruled that they had a voice in their own schools. As John Tinker declared, "I agree with Abe Fortas that we can't have a democracy without kids learning in school what freedom and democracy are about. You can't have a dictatorial approach to student expression in the schools, with the youth of the nation, and hope they will turn into democrats (with a small "d") when they are adults."

CHAPTER 4

A NEW ERA

Tinker may not have led to a "new revolutionary era of permissive-ness" as feared by Justice Hugo Black, but it certainly increased the social consciousness of many students about the importance of First Amendment freedoms and the fact that the highest court in the country had affirmed that they possessed them. In the wake of the *Tinker* decision, students challenged school policies on an assort-ment of issues, ranging from personal appearance to the distribution of newspapers to the removal of books from the school curriculum.

A prominent question on student speech rights was the applica-tion of the *Tinker* "substantial disruption" standard. What exactly must school officials show in order to justify silencing student speech in the name of disruption or interference? The answer to that ques-tion would be anything but clear.

REBEL FLAG

A prime example of the difficulty in applying the *Tinker* "substantial disruption" test occurred in Chattanooga, Tennessee, where the pub-lic high schools were in the process of being integrated. While the U.S. Supreme Court had declared segregated public schools to be in violation of the Equal Protection Clause in *Brown v. Board of Educa-tion* (1954), the Court issued another opinion the next year in the same case ordering that schools be desegregated with "all deliberate speed." Predictably, there was much more emphasis placed on the adjective "deliberate" than the noun "speed." In fact, it took nearly two decades to desegregate some public school systems in the South.

Brainerd High School in Chattanooga, Tennessee, an all-white school until 1966, had adopted the nickname "the Rebels" and used the Confederate battle flag as its school flag. During the 1969–70 school year, racial tension surfaced at the school over the continued use of the nickname *Rebel* and the song "Dixie" at various school events. In May 1970, school officials decided that the Confederate flag, the word *Rebel*, and the song "Dixie" had contributed to the racial tension at school and barred the flag and the song from school-related events. The school board then adopted a measure providing that "provocative symbols on clothing will not be allowed." The board further clarified that the Confederate flag and Confederate soldier "cannot be used as symbols for any public school in Chattanooga."

Despite the board's clear prohibition against it, Brainerd High student Rod Melton wore a jacket with an emblem of the Confederate flag to school. Eventually, school officials suspended Melton for wearing his jacket multiple times. Melton then filed a federal lawsuit, contending that the school policy banning "provocative symbols" was too vague and that he merely wore the Confederate flag as a measure of his pride in his southern heritage. The federal district court agreed that the ban on "provocative symbols" was too vague but still upheld the discipline because the wearing of the Confederate flag could cause disruption at the school, which had experienced racial tension. The district judge noted that there was not only disruption but "disorder" at the school in part as a result of the Confederate flag.

Melton appealed and a divided three-judge panel of the U.S. Court of Appeals for the Sixth Circuit agreed with the school in a 2–1 opinion in *Melton v. Young* (1972). The appeals court applied the "leading" case of *Tinker*, agreeing with the lower court that there was sufficient evidence of disruption (a leading case is one that carries much weight with other courts; in legal terms it is valuable precedent). The appeals court majority, in an opinion written by Judge Damon Keith cited a passage from the lower court that noted the school was closed on two different days because of the racially charged atmosphere.

Judge William E. Miller dissented, though he also evaluated the case through the prism of the *Tinker* "substantial disruption" test: "It is my firm conviction that the Principal in suspending the student simply over-reacted and was motivated by the kind of 'undifferentiated fear or apprehension of disturbance' which the court in Tinker held to be insufficient to overcome the right to freedom of expression." Miller distinguished between the school's use of Confederate symbols and the "small sleeve insignia" worn by a "single student." He also noted that nearly all the disruptions occurred because of school sponsorship of racially charged symbols, not individual acts by students.

The regulation of Confederate flag symbols and clothing was not unique to Tennessee. In Escambia County, Florida, school officials instituted a complete ban on all Confederate and Rebel symbols when racial disturbances occurred three years after integration. Evidence showed that black students protested the use of the term *Rebels* and the display of the Confederate flag on school premises. The school then instituted a complete prohibition against these symbols whether displayed by the school or individual students. A federal district court upheld the ban, finding that it was necessary to combat the racial tension in the school district. A three-judge panel of the U.S. Court of Appeals for the Fifth Circuit ruled in *Augustus v. School Board of Escambia County* (1975) that the lower court should have considered a less speech-restrictive alternative to a complete prohibition on the Confederate symbol. The appeals court reasoned that the lower court should have considered the option of prohibiting only the "misuse" of such symbols, such as displaying the symbols to harass or antagonize other students. Judge Leonard Moore warned in his separate dissenting opinion that the majority's opinion exemplified what he called a "tyranny of the courts" and that the federal courts cannot "substitute themselves for big brother" in George Orwell's "prophetic novel fast becoming nonfiction."

The *Melton* and *Augustus* cases show courts grappling with how to deal with environments tinged with racial hostility just a few years removed from integration. School officials had a duty to ensure that students—often a small minority of African American students—were protected from violence. Still, today such controversies occur in many states, not just the southern states, when students wear Confederate flag clothing to school. Some school districts have imposed a flat ban on the controversial symbol, believing that it naturally exacerbates racial tensions and leads to interracial violence.

HAIR

As with clothing concerns, students across the country began to assert their independence and question school rules related to hair. The 1960s and 1970s were a time when many teens experimented with their appearance, with many young men letting their hair grow quite long. Often identified as part of the "hippie" movement, long hair was viewed by many school officials as an embodiment of the disorder, disruption, and decadence that the excesses of some demonstrations on college campuses had produced.

As a result, many school districts across the country passed grooming regulations that specifically forbade the wearing of long hair by boys. Many students suspended or otherwise punished under such policies sued in court, contending that these rules violated either their free expression rights under the First Amendment or their liberty interest under the Due Process Clause of the Fourteenth Amendment. These long-hair cases flooded the courts, with surprisingly varied results.

Some courts viewed such measures as a direct violation of either the First Amendment or due process. In *Holsapple v. Woods* (1974), a panel of the U.S. Court of Appeals for the Seventh Circuit upheld a lower court ruling that invalidated the suspension of student Lowell F. Holsapple for wearing long hair to Odin High School in

Odin, Illinois. His school had instituted a rule that read: "Excessively long hair to the eyebrows, ears, and to the collar will be cause for dismissal." School officials presented the testimony of four expert witnesses—all experienced educators and administrators—who testified that there was a correlation between long hair and poor school performance. One expert, a professor of school administration at Eastern Illinois University, said that students with long hair generally caused discipline problems at the college level. Another expert witness said that students with long hair generally were academic underachievers. Despite this litany of supposed "expert" testimony, a federal district court ruled in favor of young Holsapple, a finding affirmed by the Seventh Circuit. The court noted that "the right to wear one's hair at any length or in any desired manner is an ingredient of personal freedom protected by the United States Constitution."

The courts disagreed over whether the liberty of students to grow their hair as they saw fit was moored in the First Amendment or the Due Process Clause of the Fourteenth Amendment, which protects life, liberty, and property interests from unreasonable government interference. Many courts believed that the right to grow long hair was a liberty interest within the meaning of the Due Process Clause. In *Massie v. Henry* (1972), the U.S. Court of Appeals for the Fourth Circuit ruled that a lower court made a mistake in dismissing a group of students' constitutional claims challenging a policy limiting the length of hair and sideburns. The school had argued that having long hair created safety concerns, even going so far as to have a welding instructor testify that sparks from tools could light students' long hair on fire.

The Fourth Circuit, however, noted that many of their law clerks—the young attorneys who serve under judges for a year or two—had long hair. They pointed out that numerous presidents had long hair or mustaches, including Benjamin Harrison, Grover Cleveland, Theodore Roosevelt, and William Howard Taft. The court even invoked the name of Jesus, writing: "Although there exists no depiction of Jesus Christ, either reputedly or historically accurate, he has always been shown with hair at least the length of that of plaintiffs."

Other courts, however, gave very short shrift to students' First Amendment claims to wear hairstyles of their choice. Robert Olff found this out the hard way when he and his mother challenged the policy of East Side Union High School District in San Jose, California. The policy provided: "Hair shall be trim and clean. A boy's hair shall not fall below the eyes in front and shall not cover the ears, and it shall not extend below the collar in back." Both a federal district court and a federal appeals court rejected his constitutional challenge. Olff appealed to the U.S. Supreme Court, pointing out that the lower courts were deeply divided over these "hair cases." The U.S. Supreme Court refused to hear the case, though Justice William O. Douglas dissented from this refusal (known in the law as a "denial of certiorari") in *Olff v. East Side Union High School* (1972). He wrote: "It seems incredible that under our federalism a State can deny a student education in its public school system unless his hair style comports with the standards of the school board. Some institutions in Asia require their enrollees to shave their heads. Would we sustain that regulation if imposed by a public school? Would we sustain a public school regulation requiring male students to have crew cuts?"

The hair cases of the 1970s showed that more and more students were willing to challenge school officials by asserting their constitutional rights. The *Tinker* case had ushered in a new era of litigiousness, if not permissiveness.

DEMONSTRATIONS

Students believed that the promise of *Tinker* extended to more than choice of clothing or hair style. Some also believed that it should protect their right to protest. Steven Karp was one of these students.

In 1971, Karp and several other students at Canyon del Oro High School in Pima County, Arizona, believed that school officials made a grievous mistake in failing to renew the teaching contract of a certain English teacher. The students decided to stage a walkout at

an athletic banquet ceremony to protest the decision. They had contacted members of the local news media to publicize their walkout. A
local newspaper covered the pending student demonstration. When
several student athletes threatened physical violence if such a demonstration occurred, school officials canceled the banquet. However,
several students still staged a walkout from classes, and later in the
day some students began displaying signs protesting the firing of
the teacher. School officials sought to shut down the protest by gath-
ering all the signs. Karp went out to his car to grab his sign. He initially refused to give his sign to the vice principal, as the school had
no official rule banning signs. The resulting demonstration occurred
but was eventually broken up by school officials. Those officials later
imposed a five-day suspension on Karp, saying they would reduce
the suspension to three days if he would agree to quit bringing signs
to campus. Karp later sued, contending that school officials violated
his First Amendment rights. A federal district court ruled in favor of
school officials, reasoning that the actions of Karp helped contribute
to the disruptive demonstration that interrupted the school day.

On appeal, a three-judge panel of the U.S. Court of Appeals for
the Ninth Circuit reversed the lower court ruling in *Karp v. Becken*
(1973). The court struggled with application of the Supreme Court's
decision in *Tinker*. "The Tinker rule is simply stated; application,
however, is more difficult," Judge J. Clifford Wallace wrote for the
panel. "Federal courts should treat the Tinker rule as a flexible one
dependent upon the totality of relevant facts in each case."

Under *Tinker*, school officials do not have to wait for an actual
disruption to occur; however, they must show "the existence of facts
which might reasonably lead [them] to forecast substantial disruption." The federal district court had found that there were enough
factors showing a reasonable forecast of disruption, including the
threats of retaliatory violence by school athletes, the cancellation
of the assembly because of a fear of violence, the actual walking out
of class by numerous students, and the pulling of a fire alarm by one
student demonstrator.

However, the appeals court ruled that there were still questions to be answered as to the punishment of Karp merely for displaying his sign. "The sign activity in this case constituted the exercise of pure speech rather than conduct," Wallace wrote. Furthermore, the school had no rule prohibiting students from possessing signs. The court found that school officials failed to justify punishing Karp merely for displaying signs in connection with the demonstration. "What we have said does not mean that the school officials could not have suspended appellant [Karp] for violating an existing reasonable rule," the court wrote. "In fact, in securing the signs, he broke a regulation by going to the parking lot during school hours. However, this was not a basis of the suspension."

Other student demonstration cases during the post-*Tinker* period generally gave deference to school officials. Courts reasoned that mass student demonstrations and exodus from classes constituted a direct disruption of and interference with school activities. For example, nearly three hundred African American students participated in a "mass action protest" at John Tyler High School in Tyler, Texas, after school officials instituted a policy that led to the selection of more white than black cheerleaders. The U.S. Court of Appeals for the Fifth Circuit in *Dunn v. Tyler Independent School District* (1972) contrasted the passive wearing of black armbands with disruptive action and group demonstrations that involved a number of students.

School officials of the era showed little tolerance for mass student protests or demonstrations. They often claimed such protests caused disruptions or otherwise intruded on the learning process. Judges normally deferred to the day-to-day judgments of school administrators. The First Amendment allows individuals to march and protest against government policies with which they disagree. But the "special characteristics" of the school environment mentioned by Justice Fortas in the *Tinker* case normally prohibit such action in schools. It was one of the classic disconnects between the First Amendment in secondary schools and in society at large.

REGULATING STUDENT NEWSPAPERS
Some of the most controversial and important student speech controversies in the 1970s and early 1980s concerned the regulation of

student newspapers—both official school publications and so-called "underground" student newspapers. Student journalists believed that they had the right to cover topics of interest to them, such as sex and drugs. School officials countered that some of these subjects were inappropriate for minors. Often courts didn't provide much protection to student journalists, particularly those who created their own underground newspapers.

Gregory Williams served as the student editor of the *Joint Effort* at Springbrook High School in Montgomery County, Maryland. Williams's paper didn't shy away from covering issues related to marijuana, something that displeased school officials, who had initially approved the distribution of the paper but then balked when they saw it. The building monitor, Austin Patterson, saw that he was the subject of a cartoon in the paper that showed him dressed as a sheriff in Western garb, saying, "DON' SMOKE DAT EVIL WEED, I'LL BUST YO ASS!" Another part of the paper featured an ad for the Earthworks Headshop, which sold drug paraphernalia. The principal ordered the seizure of all copies of the paper. The U.S. Court of Appeals for the Fourth Circuit in *Williams v. Spencer* (1980) held that school officials could halt distribution of any student publication—school sponsored or otherwise—that encouraged actions that endangered the health or safety of students.

Jeff Trachtman, senior editor of the *Stuyvesant Voice* at Stuyvesant High School in New York, also found out that there was a limit on content for his newspaper. Trachtman helped compose a questionnaire meant to collect information on the attitudes of students toward sex. The survey covered such topics as premarital sex, contraception, homosexuality, masturbation, and the extent of students' sexual experiences. The survey included a caveat: "You are not required to answer any of the questions and if you feel particularly uncomfortable—don't push yourself." School officials, however, would not allow the survey or the planned article, which would feature its results, to be distributed.

Trachtman sued, contending a violation of First Amendment rights. The school officials countered with affidavits from four experts, psychologists and psychiatrists, who testified that many adolescents would be harmed or made to feel anxious by answering such questions. Plaintiffs countered with five experts of their own, including Jeff's father, Gilbert, who was a professor of educational psychology at New York University. The plaintiffs' experts testified that the survey could be of substantial benefit to many students. The federal district court and the reviewing Second Circuit in *Tracht-man v. Anker* (1977) determined that there was the potential for some ninth- and tenth-graders to suffer emotional harm from answering these questions. "We believe that school authorities did not act unreasonably in deciding that the proposed questionnaire should not be distributed because of the probability that it would result in psychological harm to some students," the court wrote. "The First Amendment right to express one's views does not include the right to importune others to respond to questions when there is reason to believe that such importuning may result in harmful consequences."

Yet not all courts ruled against students' efforts to produce and distribute either controversial or underground newspapers at school. In *Thomas v. Board of Education, Granville Central School District* (1979), the Second Circuit ruled that school officials at Granville Junior-Senior High School in Granville, New York, exceeded their authority and violated the First Amendment when they prohibited students from publishing *Hard Times*. The newspaper featured articles on masturbation, prostitution, and other controversial topics. However, students produced the paper off campus and distributed it outside of school. Even though they distributed the paper off campus, they had received school suspensions.

The court believed that the school exceeded its authority in regulating what was essentially an off-campus paper. "When school officials are authorized only to punish speech on school property, the student is free to speak his mind when the school day ends." The court said that officials had also failed to show how an off-campus student newspaper negatively impacted discipline at school.

Not every case involved the censorship of papers that discussed drugs or sex. Sometimes the issue boiled down to whether school officials should have the power to review student newspapers before they were printed. Student advocates contended that this type of prepublication review amounted to a prior restraint on expression, a twentieth-century version of the infamous English licensing laws of the seventeenth century, which required printers to obtain government approval before printing. It was those laws that caused English poet John Milton to pen his memorable tract *Areopagitica* defending freedom of expression. School officials, however, didn't care about lofty language from 1644; they wanted to ensure order in the schools and cut down on supposedly disruptive influences. Some courts held that such review was a classic prior restraint on expression, anathema to fundamental First Amendment principles. Other courts determined that such policies were necessary in order to ensure that the material being distributed was not harmful to other students. School officials justified their actions by asserting that they were protecting other young students, pointing out that even in high schools some of the students are only fourteen years old. While some of the student publications pushed the boundaries of good taste, many of them discussed issues relevant to young people, including sex, drugs, and music.

The reality was that students too often did not receive the freedom they wanted or needed to cover controversial issues in schools. Pulitzer Prize–winning reporter Jack Nelson captured this dilemma for students well in his aptly titled book *Captive Voices* (1974). His report eventually led to the creation of the Student Press Law Center, which still tirelessly advocates today on behalf of student journalists.

BOOK BANNING

Given the various conflicts over student dress, hair, and newspapers in the post-*Tinker* days, one would have thought the Supreme Court would address these contentious areas but it didn't. As a result, conflicting rulings by lower courts led to confusion among school officials and students over the level of free speech protection for various types of expression.

The Supreme Court did intervene in another contentious area

in the schools—the removal of books from school libraries that some parents or school officials might deem objectionable or inappropriate. The question of what books are educationally suitable for children still divides school districts, parents, librarians, teachers, communities, and even Supreme Court justices. Eventually the Court decided a case (albeit on very narrow grounds) that provided at least some guidance.

The stage was set for eventual Supreme Court review because lower courts disagreed mightily over how to assess book-banning controversies. In *Minarcini v. Strongsville City School District* (1976), the U.S. Court of Appeals for the Sixth Circuit determined that school officials from Strongsville, Ohio, violated the First Amendment when they removed copies of *Catch-22* by Joseph Heller and two of Kurt Vonnegut's books from the school curriculum and the library shelves. "A library is a storehouse of knowledge," the court wrote in finding that students have the right to receive information and ideas.

Other courts, by contrast, were far less sensitive and protective. In *Bicknell v. Vergennes Union High School Bd.* (1979), a federal district court in Vermont upheld the right of school officials to remove books from the library shelves. The reasoning of the court was that the students could access the books at public libraries or purchase copies from a bookstore. "Students remain free to purchase the books in question from private bookstores, to read them in other libraries, to carry them to school and to discuss them freely during the school day. Neither the Board's failure to purchase a work nor its decision to remove or restrict access to a work in the school library violate the First Amendment rights of the student plaintiffs before this court."

In 1982, a long-pending and significant book-banning case reached the U.S. Supreme Court. The Board of Education of the Island Trees Union Free School District No. 26 in New York had determined in 1976 that several books should be removed from the libraries of Island Trees High School and Island Trees Memorial Junior High School. The titles included

The Adventures of Huckleberry Finn (Mark Twain)
Slaughterhouse-Five (Kurt Vonnegut)
The Naked Ape (Desmond Morris)
Down These Mean Streets (Piri Thomas)
Best Short Stories of Negro Writers (ed. Langston Hughes)
Go Ask Alice ("Anonymous")
Laughing Boy (Oliver LaFarge)
Black Boy (Richard Wright)
A Hero Ain't Nothing but a Sandwich (Alice Childress)
Soul on Ice (Eldridge Cleaver)

The school board appointed a book-review committee, which recommended that only two of the books—*The Naked Ape* and *Down These Mean Streets*—be removed. The school board rejected the committee's recommendations, saying it had the moral duty to protect children. Several members of the board described the books as "anti-American, anti-Christian, anti-Semitic and just plain filthy." Four high school students (Steven Pico, Jacqueline Gold, Glenn Yarris, and Russell Rieger) and one junior high school student (Paul Sochinski) challenged the school board's actions in federal court, contending that those actions violated the First Amendment. "The first time I learned about the book censorship was at a school assembly when my English teacher, Mrs. Pepper, whispered in my ear, 'Did you know that books are being removed from the library?'" Rieger recalled in an interview. "I couldn't believe that they were taking away classics from the library. I was also told that they removed the books at night when no one was around."

In 1979, a federal district court ruled for the school board, determining that the removal of the books did not raise a First Amendment issue. "While removal of such books from a school library may . . . reflect a misguided educational philosophy, it does not constitute a sharp and direct infringement of any First Amendment rights."

The district court determined that federal judges should not normally intervene in the daily operations of schools unless "basic constitutional values" were "sharply implicated." A three-judge panel of the U.S. Court of Appeals for the Second Circuit reversed the district court, finding that the students should have been given an opportunity to prove that the justifications for book removals were "simply pretexts for the suppression of free speech," as the students alleged.

The case proceeded to the U.S. Supreme Court, which ruled on June 25, 1982, in *Board of Education v. Pico* in favor of the students. Writing for the plurality, Justice William Brennan wrote that "the First Amendment rights of students may be directly and sharply implicated by the removal of books from the shelves of a school library."

Brennan emphasized that the First Amendment protects the right of students to "receive information and ideas" and recognized that "the school library is the principal locus of such freedom." He determined that whether the removal of the books violated the First Amendment depended upon the motivation for the school board's actions. He explained that school boards could remove books they thought were "pervasively vulgar" or educationally unsuitable. However, school boards could not remove books simply because they disagreed with the ideas conveyed in those books. Brennan wrote: "In brief, we hold that local school boards may not remove books from school library shelves simply because they dislike the ideas contained in those books and seek by their removal to 'prescribe what shall be orthodox in politics, nationalism, religion, or other matters of public opinion.'"

Four justices dissented, including then associate justice William Rehnquist and Sandra Day O'Connor, the first woman appointed to the Court. The dissenters described Brennan's opinion as a "lavish expansion" of the Court's First Amendment jurisprudence. They reasoned that it would force federal courts to become "super censors" of school boards and that having federal judges second-guessing school boards' reasons for rejecting books would hamper the boards' ability to inculcate fundamental values.

The impact of the *Pico* decision is debatable. First, Justice Brennan's opinion was only a plurality and did not command five votes on the Court. Justice Byron White concurred only in the result. Additionally, Justice Brennan's opinion dealt only with the narrow issue of removing books from school libraries, not acquiring books or even removing them from classroom reading lists. The Court did not rule that school officials could never remove books from library shelves. The Court only said that school officials couldn't remove books because they disagreed with the ideas in those books. On the other hand, *Pico* stands as an important First Amendment precedent and a victory for student expression. "We overcame the substantial hurdle when the Court rejected the school board's argument that the school board's control over library books posed no First Amendment issue," said Arthur Eisenberg of the New York Civil Liberties Union, who was one of the attorneys for the students in the case. "The *Pico* case is significant because it resisted the oversimplified claim advanced by the school board that because the school board buys the books, they have the authority to determine what books are on the library shelves without First Amendment concerns," Eisenberg said.

It also had an important impact for Steven Pico, Russell Rieger, and the other students involved, because a year after the Supreme Court's decision the school board voted 4–3 to restore the books to the shelves.

The Court's decision in *Pico* has not ended the censorship of books, which is alive and well. There were 513 challenges to books in 2008 and 460 challenges to books in 2009, according to the American Library Association. Books are most frequently banned when they contain controversial language or deal with sexuality, race, the occult, illegal drugs, suicide, and violence. In an effort to shield children from material they consider questionable, parents and school board members have advocated the removal from schools of a variety of books, including literary classics such as *Catch-22* by Joseph Heller and *I Know Why the Caged Bird Sings* by Maya Angelou. The successful Harry Potter series by J.K. Rowling has incited controversy all over the country. Parents from Minnesota to South Carolina have asked school officials to remove wizard Harry from shelves because the books allegedly promote the occult.

·   ·   ·

The post-*Tinker* period of the 1970s witnessed an explosion of student litigation on a variety of issues. The Supreme Court's decision in *Tinker* created a possibility for students to assert their free speech rights in different contexts. Students and student advocates felt encouraged by the Supreme Court's admonition that students don't "shed their constitutional rights to freedom of speech and expression at the schoolhouse gate." The tenor of the times contributed to this sense of opportunity for students.

But the 1980s weren't so propitious for student rights.

CHAPTER 5

SUPREME RETRACTIONS

The *Tinker* decision ushered in a new era for student speech, setting a formidable hurdle for school officials to clear before silencing student speakers. The absolute authority of school officials faced opposition from the highest court in the land. No longer could officials shut down student speech merely on command, as they had for centuries. Now, they often had to show that the student speech would cause a substantial disruption or material interference with school activities.

The *Tinker* decision was a product of its time—the late 1960s and early 1970s. It was an era of social rebellion when youth protestors stood at the vanguard of social change, using their voices to urge various forms of social change. Young people across the country questioned the conservative social agendas established by authority figures.

Society changed in the 1980s, retreating from some of the perceived excesses of the sixties and seventies. Attitudes became more restrained in many circles, and the U.S. Supreme Court became more conservative with the addition of new justices. The 1960s had featured a relatively liberal Supreme Court headed by Chief Justice Earl Warren. Democratic presidents John F. Kennedy and Lyndon Johnson had appointed more liberal justices, something that President Richard M. Nixon did not do. Nixon, an attorney educated at Duke Law School who had argued a First Amendment case before the United States Supreme Court in *Time v. Hill* (1967), believed that the Warren Court had gone too far in expanding individuals' constitutional rights. Upon Warren's retirement, he appointed a law-and-order federal appeals court jurist named Warren Burger. It was an appointment that would prove significant for many areas of law, including student speech.

Because the Supreme Court decided not to address student speech cases for years, student speech law developed in the lower courts. The Court finally decided the *Pico* book censorship case in 1982, but that was a very narrow, fractured decision. It was not until several years later that the Court returned to the subject of student speech, in the last year of Chief Justice Burger's tenure, in a rather unusual case involving a bold young teenager named Matthew Fraser.

TO THE CLIMAX

In April 1983, seventeen-year-old Matthew Fraser, a senior at Bethel High School in Pierce County, Washington, delivered an unforgettable speech nominating his classmate Jeff Kuhlman for student body vice president. Fraser was not only a member of the school's honor society but also the star of the debate team. He had even earned the "Top Speaker" award in state debate tournaments for two years running. Fellow students and others paid attention when Fraser spoke. Standing before an assembly of more than six hundred students, Fraser delivered a memorable speech in support of Kuhlman:

> I know a man who is firm—he's firm in his pants, he's firm in his shirt, his character is firm—but most . . . of all, his belief in you, the students of Bethel, is firm.
>
> Jeff Kuhlman is a man who takes his point and pounds it in. If necessary, he'll take an issue and nail it to the wall. He doesn't attack things in spurts—he drives hard, pushing and pushing until finally—he succeeds.
>
> Jeff is a man who will go to the very end—even the climax, for each and every one of you.
>
> So vote for Jeff for A.S.B. vice-president—he'll never come between you and the best our high school can be.

The speech, with its obvious and frequent sexual references, drew hooting and hollering from some in the student body. "I wrote the speech about an hour before the assembly," Fraser said. "One teacher told me it would 'raise some eyebrows.' But no teacher told me that I violated school policy." In later court testimony, Fraser said that he gave the speech "to humor his audience" so they would vote for his candidate. Fraser's plan worked, as Kuhlman won the vice presidency.

The day after the speech, an assistant principal called Fraser into her office and informed him that he had violated the following school rule: "Conduct which materially and substantially interferes with the educational process is prohibited, including the use of obscene, profane language or gestures." The assistant principal gave Fraser copies of letters from five teachers opposing his speech. Fraser admitted he delivered the speech with sexual innuendo and received a three-day suspension. Additionally, the assistant principal said that Fraser would be removed from a list of possible student speakers at graduation.

Fraser appealed his suspension through the school grievance procedure to no avail. The grievance hearing officer determined that the speech was "indecent, lewd and obscene" and merited punishment. Fraser served two days of the suspension before being allowed to return to school. Undeterred, Fraser sued in federal court, alleging a violation of his First Amendment rights. He challenged the school's disruptive-conduct rule as overbroad and vague.

A federal district court judge ruled in Fraser's favor, determining that school officials violated not only his First Amendment rights by punishing him for the content of his speech but also violated his due process rights by removing him from the list of possible graduation speakers. The judge noted that the school failed to provide notice that a person could be removed from the list of graduation speakers merely for violating the no-disruptive-language rule. The judge awarded Fraser $278 in damages and more than $12,000 in litigation costs and attorneys fees.

After the punishment and court victory, Fraser became a cult hero in school. His fellow students selected him by write-in vote to speak at graduation. "The school officials martyred me," he said.

"There were football players in the school who made signs saying 'Stand firm for Matt.'"

School officials appealed the decision to the U.S. Court of Appeals for the Ninth Circuit. They advanced three arguments justifying the suspension of Fraser: (1) the speech had a disruptive impact upon the student assembly and the school; (2) the school officials had an interest in maintaining civility in school; and (3) school officials have greater authority to regulate student speech that is school sponsored.

The school pressed hard on the disruption issue, arguing that school officials must have the ability to prohibit such student speech. The school had emphasized the deposition testimony of a school counselor who talked about a group of students "hooting and hollering" after the speech. However, the school counselor also said that the reaction was not that much different from any high school student assembly. The officials also cited the testimony of another teacher who witnessed other students engaged in "loud clapping, hoots and hollering." Finally, they mentioned the testimony of a home economics teacher who devoted ten minutes of her class the next morning to address the controversy.

The Ninth Circuit issued a 2–1 decision that affirmed the lower court decision and ruled in favor of Matthew Fraser. The majority, in an opinion by Judge William Norris, wrote that none of this testimony showed that there was any real disruption of school activities. The school assembly started and finished on time. "Given the evidence before us, we fail to see how we can distinguish this case from *Tinker* on the issue of disruption," Norris wrote. "Just as the record in *Tinker* failed to yield evidence that the wearing of black armbands resulted in a material interference with school activity, the record now before us yields no evidence that Fraser's use of a sexual innuendo in his speech materially interfered with activities at Bethel High School. While the students' reaction to Fraser's speech may fairly be characterized as boisterous, it was hardly disruptive of the educational process." The school officials repeatedly had characterized Fraser's speech as "inappropriate" rather than disruptive. They then self-servingly, during litigation, seemed to equate inappropriate with disruptive. The Ninth Circuit panel majority was having none of it, writing: "The First Amendment standard *Tinker* requires us to apply is material disruption, not inappropriateness."

Norris then addressed the school district's argument that it must have the ability to protect other students—most of them minors—from offensive or indecent speech. The district relied in part on the Supreme Court's decision in *FCC v. Pacifica Foundation* (1978) in which the Court ruled that the Federal Communications Commission could discipline a radio station for playing comedian George Carlin's "Filthy Words" monologue during daytime hours when children were apt to be listening. The district also relied on Judge Jon O. Newman's statement in a student underground newspaper case in which he wrote: "If the F.C.C. can act to keep indecent language off the afternoon airwaves, a school can act to keep indecent language from circulating on high school grounds."

However, Norris was not buying the analogy to *Pacifica* because a major reason for limiting indecent speech over the broadcast medium of radio was protecting privacy of the home from offensive, unwanted expression. He noted that the privacy rationale was inapplicable in a school assembly. "High school students voluntarily attending an assembly to hear student campaign speeches surely do not expect the same measure of privacy and protection from unwelcome language and ideas that they obviously do at home," Norris wrote. "A high school assembly is a very public place." The other major rationale of the *Pacifica* decision was that indecent language on the broadcast medium could reach impressionable young children. The Ninth Circuit found this inapplicable to the *Fraser* case because Matthew Fraser was speaking to teenagers, not young children. "Realistically, high school students are beyond the point of being sheltered from the potpourri of sights and sounds we encounter at every turn in our daily lives," the court wrote. "We fear that if school officials had the unbridled discretion to apply a standard as subjective and elusive as 'indecency' in controlling the speech of high school students, it would increase the risk of cementing white, middle-class standards for determining what is acceptable and proper speech and behavior in our public schools."

Finally, the school district argued that Fraser's speech occurred as part of a school assembly, a form of school-sponsored speech akin to the school curriculum covered in classrooms. The Ninth Circuit did not accept this analogy either, noting that the assembly was a voluntary event and that students could have attended study hall instead if they chose.

The Ninth Circuit concluded that as long as Fraser's speech was not obscene or disruptive, he had the right to say what he wanted at the assembly. Fraser's speech was vulgar, but it did not rise of the level of obscenity—a category of speech reserved for hard-core pornography.

Reflecting on the case, Jeffrey T. Haley, who represented Fraser, wryly observed: "I wish perhaps I had asked the Ninth Circuit not to rule so strongly in our favor." Haley said this because he realized that the U.S. Supreme Court might think the Ninth Circuit had gone too far in protecting student speech.

Judge Eugene Wright, appointed to the "liberal" Ninth Circuit by President Richard Nixon, issued a strong dissent, reminiscent of Justice Black's dissent in *Tinker*. "I dissent because the majority improperly usurps the authority of school officials to maintain and enforce minimum standards of decency in public schools."

Wright's dissent and the possible overreach of the majority opinion encouraged the district to pursue Supreme Court review. William Coats, who represented the school district, believed in the principle that schools should be able to punish students for indecent speech. "We were never looking for a test case," he said. "The case occurred because of one phone call I got a call from a school official saying, 'We had a student give a lewd speech before a student assembly. Can we discipline him?' I said 'yes.'"

The Supreme Court heard oral arguments in the case in March 1986. Coats, representing the school district, explained in his opening statement that Fraser had given a "crude and vulgar speech." He then contrasted Fraser's speech with the symbolic speech in *Tinker*. According to Coats, there was nothing "intrinsically harmful" about the speech in *Tinker*. He also contended that the Court ruled in favor of the *Tinker* participants because there was evidence of discrimination against a particular political viewpoint. In the *Fraser* case, Coats argued, school officials weren't engaging in viewpoint discrimination; they just wanted to prohibit vulgar and lewd talk. He also argued that the other students in the audience were a "captive audience," unlike the situation in *Tinker*.

When Fraser's attorney, Jeffrey Haley, approached the lectern for his turn at oral argument, justices peppered him with sharp questions over whether school officials can regulate obscene or profane speech. They blitzed him with several hypotheticals, asking whether the school could have disciplined Matthew Fraser if he had uttered a string of curse words. Haley emphasized that the speech did not cause any disruption of school activities: "The sexual metaphor that was used in this speech was not in any way intended to insult or create divisiveness between students or cause any disruption, and the record shows that there was no disruption." Haley also noted the success of Fraser's speech in helping to get his classmate elected and that "sex is not a forbidden topic" among students.

Justice Lewis Powell then questioned Haley as to whether Fraser's speech was a form of political speech.

POWELL:	Do you think this was political speech?
HALEY:	It is very much a political speech.
POWELL:	It's a student political campaign, but it's nothing like the speech in *Tinker*, which really related to politics. Here, do you think the words that are particularly involved had anything to do with the political campaign?
HALEY:	The messages that he conveyed, the content, which included sexual allusions, was part of a political speech.

Haley even argued that students in literature classes were exposed to more explicit descriptions of sex when they read Shakespeare. "Romeo and Juliet is a standard text within the classes and there are sexual allusions and metaphors in Romeo and Juliet that are more explicit, that are actually describing sexual activity."

In the last opinion of the term—issued on July 7, 1986—Chief Justice Warren Burger wrote the final opinion of his judicial career, *Bethel School District No. 403 v. Fraser.* It was a momentous one for school officials and student speech law alike.

Burger emphasized the "marked distinction" between the "political message" in *Tinker* and the "sexual content" of Fraser's speech. He articulated a balance between freedom of speech and the teaching of core values: "The undoubted freedom to advocate unpopular and controversial views in schools and classrooms must be balanced against the society's countervailing interest in teaching students the boundaries of socially appropriate behavior."

He relied in part on a decision that the Court had issued the previous term involving a Fourth Amendment search and seizure case in public schools—*New Jersey v. T.L.O.* (1985). In the New Jersey case, the Court had rejected a Fourth Amendment challenge to a search of a female student's purse by an assistant principal with less than probable cause. In its decision, the Court had said that the rights of minors are not "automatically coextensive" with that of adults. Burger cited that passage from *T.L.O.* in his *Fraser* opinion and added that "schools must teach by example the shared values of a civilized social order." He then established what became known as the "Fraser standard": "Surely it is a highly appropriate function of public school education to prohibit the use of vulgar and offensive terms in public discourse." He added that school officials can prohibit "lewd, indecent or offensive speech and conduct such as that indulged in by this confused boy." Finally, Burger stressed that this was simply a case of punishing lewd and indecent speech, not of silencing a particular political viewpoint.

Even Justice William Brennan—normally a free speech stalwart on the Court—concurred with the majority's determination and ruled against Matthew Fraser. He said that Fraser had engaged in "disruptive language."

Only Justices Thurgood Marshall and John Paul Stevens sided

with Fraser. Marshall wrote that school administrators failed to present enough evidence of disruption, while Stevens focused upon the due process problems with punishing Fraser for conduct that he did not know violated school policy. Stevens began his opinion with the memorable line delivered by Clark Gable in *Gone With the Wind*: "Frankly, my dear, I don't give a damn." He reasoned that if a student is to be punished for speech, "he is entitled to fair notice of the scope of the prohibition and the consequences of its violation."

Of course Coats believed that the Court and Chief Justice Burger had delivered the right message. "School officials have the responsibility to maintain an atmosphere that is conducive to the school setting," he said. Schools have to maintain order and control and school officials can teach students proper decorum in different settings."

The *Fraser* decision represented a significant step away from the protections of *Tinker*. Burger's opinion showed a strong deference to school officials akin to the early days of the twentieth century. "It is a façade that the courts protect student rights," Fraser said fifteen years after the decision in 2001. "As a practical matter, school administrators do what they want to do." Many students today would echo that sentiment.

HAZELWOOD AND THE CENSORED ARTICLES

If the Matthew Fraser case sent a warning shot, the case of Cathy Kuhlmeier sounded the potential death knell for student rights. The case began during the 1982–1983 academic year at Hazelwood East High School in St. Louis, Missouri. Robert Stergos served as the acting faculty advisor for the *Spectrum*, the student newspaper produced as part of the high school's advanced journalism class. The *Spectrum* was published six times during the school year and typically featured stories on sports and the prom, movie reviews, and assorted other items of interest to the student body. Stergos had approved several ideas for an upcoming issue including stories about teenage pregnancy, personal interviews with three pregnant students, problems with divorce, teenage marriages, why teenagers run away from home, and one about proposed federal legislation that would limit funding for abortions. One article, written by student Shari Gordon, was entitled "Divorce's Impact on Kids May Have Life Long Affect [*sic*]." It included quoted statements from a few students about their parents.

The students wrote the articles and sent the May 1983 issue to the printer. At that time, Stergos left the school for a job out of state and was replaced by Howard Emerson. New to this role, Emerson believed that at least some of the material needed to be run by the principal, Robert Eugene Reynolds, for approval. Reynolds balked at Shari Gordon's article on divorce and the personal accounts of three pregnant students. He ordered them deleted from the newspaper. Reynolds believed that several of the articles were "personal" and of a "highly sensitive nature." He was concerned that the six pregnant students in the school would be ostracized and worried that the story on divorce did not give parents an opportunity to respond to comments made by students in the article. This resulted in a truncated version of the newspaper—the deletion of two full pages of the six-page issue. Seven students went to Reynolds's office to protest the decision—a protest that fell on deaf ears.

Three students—Cathy Kuhlmeier, Leslie Smart, and Leanne Tippett-West—sued Hazelwood School District and several school officials in federal court, citing a violation of their First Amendment rights. Kuhlmeier was the *Spectrum*'s layout editor, and Tippett-West worked as a news feature writer, cartoonist, and photographer. Smart also worked as a writer for the paper. "A few of us contacted Mr. Stergos and he suggested we contact the American Civil Liberties Union," said Kuhlmeier years later. "We did and they told us we had a good case."

The three students argued for application of the *Tinker* "substantial disruption standard," pointing out that there was no reasonable forecast of disruption or interference with school activities as a result of any of the articles on teenage pregnancy or divorce. Lawyers for the school district countered that there was no constitutional issue because the newspaper was produced as part of the curriculum in journalism class. In January 1984, the federal district court refused to dismiss the lawsuit. U.S. district court judge John Francis Nangle reasoned that even if the matter was a curricular decision, the actions of the school officials still had to comport with constitutional standards.

The school district later filed another motion in court, arguing that the case was moot, or no longer a live controversy, because all of the student plaintiffs had graduated from school and earned the highest grades possible in the journalism class. Judge Nangle granted part of the motion but refused to dismiss the plaintiffs' claims for damages. This ruling allowed the case to proceed to a bench trial— a trial before a judge, not a jury.

Testimony at trial indicated that the students had a great deal of control over story selection for the *Spectrum*. Since 1976 the newspaper had featured stories on many controversial subjects, including teenage dating and pregnancy, race, the death penalty, drug and alcohol use, a desegregation lawsuit, religious cults, and the draft. In a 1982 issue, the *Spectrum* published the following "Statement of Policy":

> *Spectrum* is a school funded newspaper; written, edited, and designed by members of the Journalism II class with assistance of advisor Mr. Robert Stergos.
>
> *Spectrum* follows journalism guidelines that are set by *Scholastic Journalism* textbook. . . .
>
> *Spectrum*, as a student-press publication, accepts all rights implied by the First Amendment of the United States Constitution which states that: "Congress shall make no law restricting . . . or abridging the freedom of speech or the press. . . ."
>
> That this right extends to high school students was clarified in the *Tinker v. Des Moines Community School District* case in 1969. The Supreme Court of the United States ruled that neither "students nor teachers shed their constitutional rights to freedom of

speech or expression at the school house gate." Only speech that "materially and substantially interferes with the requirements of appropriate discipline" can be found unacceptable and therefore prohibited.

A related school board policy provided that "school sponsored student publications will not restrict free expression or diverse viewpoints within the rules of responsible journalism. School sponsored publications are developed within the adopted curriculum and its educational implications and regular classroom activities."

The students introduced an expert witness, Dr. Robert P. Knight, professor of journalism at the University of Missouri–Columbia. Knight testified that the articles in question were neither defamatory nor obscene. He also said that they complied with reasonable journalistic standards of fairness.

The school district responded with its own expert, as is so often the case in American jurisprudence. Whether a case is about a car accident or alleged medical malpractice, each side enlists expert testimony in an effort to persuade the judge or jury. Attorneys for the school officials presented the testimony of Martin Duggan, a former editorial-page editor for the *St. Louis Globe Democrat* and former instructor at Fontbonne College. Duggan testified that the story on divorce did not meet journalistic standards of fairness because the father of one of the students quoted in the article was not given a chance to respond to the comments attributed to his daughter. The district court gave more credence to Duggan's testimony than Knight's. "Dr. Knight is deeply and personally involved with high school press issues and his own personal interests are basically aligned with an expansion of student press rights," the judge wrote. "Mr. Duggan, on the other hand, was an objective and independent witness who was not even compensated by defendants for his testimony."

Judge Nangle then explained that there were two lines of legal authority emerging in recent years with regard to student speech: (1) student-initiated speech and (2) school-sponsored student speech.

In order to justify sanctions on student-initiated speech—such as the black armbands in the famous *Tinker* case—school officials had to meet the "substantial disruption" standard. As Judge Nangle wrote, "In the first line of cases, the free speech and press rights of students are at their apogee." Educators were given more leeway in justifying sanctions on school-sponsored student speech, with "something less than substantial disruption" required.

Judge Nangle determined that this case involved school-sponsored student speech because the student newspaper was part and parcel of the educational curriculum rather than an open or public forum in which educators had delegated substantial responsibility to the student journalists. The judge noted that the students who produced the paper received a grade and academic credit for working on it.

The judge then determined that school officials had to show a reasonable basis for censoring the school-sponsored student speech—the articles in the *Spectrum*. The court gave credence to the testimony of Principal Reynolds, including his fears about the loss of privacy and anonymity of the three pregnant teenagers who wrote accounts of their travails. He had also expressed worries about the sexual content of the pregnancy accounts and the divorce article written by Shari Gordon. The judge wrote that "there is serious doubt that the article complied with the rules of fairness which are standard in the field of journalism and which were covered in the textbook used in the Journalism II class."

The three students appealed to the U.S. Court of Appeals of the Eighth Circuit, where the three-judge panel ruled 2–1 in favor the students. The majority determined that the lower court erred in finding that the school district's actions should be evaluated only under a reasonableness standard. Instead, they found that the *Spectrum* was a public forum, mainly controlled by the students, that school officials had intentionally opened up to diverse viewpoints.

Judge Gerald W. Heaney wrote for the panel majority, "*The Spectrum* was not just a class exercise in which students learned to prepare papers and hone writing skills, it was a public forum established to give students an opportunity to express their views while gaining an appreciation of their rights and responsibilities under the First Amendment to the United States Constitution and their state constitution."

Because the newspaper was a public forum, the school officials would have to meet the *Tinker* "reasonable forecast of substantial disruption" standard in order to justify the censorship decision by Principal Reynolds. The panel majority found that "there is no evidence in this record which supports the administrators' fear that the pregnancy case study would create the impression that the school endorsed the sexual norms of the students interviewed."

Circuit Judge Roger L. Wollman dissented, reasoning that the *Spectrum* was not a public forum but a school-sponsored publication that was part of the curriculum. "It may be that the defendant school officials acted out of a too abundant sense of caution," he wrote. "We judges are not journalists, however, and even less school administrators. Granting the defendant school officials the deference due them, I would hold that they committed no constitutional violation in declining to publish the articles in question."

The school district officials appealed to the U.S. Supreme Court, hopeful that they could overcome the long odds for high court review. "You never know if the court will take your case or how they will rule, but I knew that our chances were certainly raised when the Court agreed to hear the case," recalled the school district's attorney, Robert P. Baine Jr. "We felt that we had a good argument."

Despite their optimism, the school district and Baine were concerned about the composition of the Court. Chief Justice Warren Burger had retired. President Ronald Reagan had nominated Robert Bork for the high court, but the Senate had failed to confirm him. This left a Supreme Court with only eight justices rather than the customary nine. "We were afraid of a Court ruling 4–4," Baine said. "If the Supreme Court had split 4–4, then the ruling of the Eighth Circuit against the Hazelwood School District would have stood."

The district pressed the argument that the school had greater authority over school-sponsored material and the curriculum. "The real issue in this case," Baine said, "is that the school paper produced as part of a class was a matter of the school curriculum."

The justices in turn pressed the attorneys on both sides to articulate the proper standard that the Court should apply. The Court could apply the *Tinker* substantial disruption standard, the standard from the recently decided *Fraser* case, or something else. The Court in *Hazelwood* chose something else.

The Court did not take its standard from the advocates at oral argument, or from *Tinker* or *Fraser*. Instead they took it from an unlikely source—a prisoner case. The year before, the Court had decided a case from Missouri involving an inmate named Leonard Safley who wished to marry a female inmate and send her love letters. The problem for Safley was that the Missouri Department of Corrections had rules prohibiting inmates from marrying each other and from mailing correspondence to each other for security reasons. In that decision, Justice Sandra Day O'Connor wrote in *Turner v. Safley*: "When a prison regulation impinges on inmates' constitutional rights, the regulation is valid if it is reasonably related to legitimate penological interests."

In its ruling in *Hazelwood*, the Court articulated a new standard for school-sponsored student speech that was eerily reminiscent of the standard for Leonard Safley and other prison inmates. Writing for the majority Justice Byron White wrote: "We hold that educators do not offend the First Amendment by exercising editorial control over the style and content of student speech in school-sponsored expressive activities so long as their actions are reasonably related to legitimate pedagogical concerns."

Just as the standard for prisoners' constitutional rights was "reasonably related to legitimate penological concerns," the standard for student rights was "reasonably related to legitimate pedagogical concerns." The Court simply substituted the word "pedagogical" for "penological." Put even more bluntly, the Court held that students engaging in school-sponsored speech have roughly the same level of free speech rights as prison inmates. This did not please student speech advocates, who decried the Court's decision as abject censorship.

Critics also seized upon Justice White's broad language as to what constituted a reasonable educational reason for censorship. White interpreted "reasonable educational reasons" as breathtakingly broad, including censoring any student expression "that might reasonably be perceived to advocate drug or alcohol use, irresponsible sex . . . or to associate the school with any position other than neutrality on matters of political controversy."

The Court determined that this reasonableness standard applied to all forms of school-sponsored speech unless the speech in question was part of a public forum. White reasoned that school facilities, including school newspapers, are public forums only if "by policy or by practice" school officials have opened up such facilities for "indiscriminate use by the general public" or the officials have agreed that the newspaper or other school-sponsored student speech is a public forum where students have broad control. The Court focused on the fact that students received grades and academic credit for working on the *Spectrum,* that the paper was produced within the confines of a journalism class, and that a journalism textbook was used in the class. White concluded that the newspaper was designed to be a "supervised learning experience" rather than an outlet for indiscriminate public use in which students could advocate whatever positions they wished.

Applying the deferential reasonableness standard, White then approved of the actions taken by Principal Reynolds in censoring the articles. "The girls did comment in the article, however, concerning their sexual histories and their use or nonuse of birth control," White wrote. "It was not unreasonable for the principal to have concluded that such frank talk was inappropriate in a school-sponsored publication distributed to 14-year-old freshmen and presumably taken home to be read by students' even younger brothers and sisters."

Justice Brennan, joined by Marshall and Harry Blackmun, published a stinging dissent. Brennan wrote that "the case before us aptly illustrates how readily school officials (and courts) can camouflage viewpoint discrimination as the 'mere' protection of students from sensitive topics." He accused the majority of approving of "brutal censorship." Brennan concluded: "The young men and women of Hazelwood East expected a civics lesson, but not the one the Court teaches them today."

FALLOUT

The *Hazelwood* decision was a resounding victory for school administrators and a spirit-dashing defeat for student journalists. Baine said the court majority got the case right. "This is an issue of the control of curriculum. I think that the *Tinker* case had been abused. The original basis for *Tinker* was good but some lower courts had expanded *Tinker* to the point where school officials would have had to permit the printing of anything students wrote.

"There is a saying that 'all education is local,' and I think the *Hazelwood* case stands for that principle," Baine said.

Frank Susman, who helped argue the case on behalf of the students before the Eighth Circuit but not before the Supreme Court, thought that *Hazelwood* "was the start of the downfall for student First Amendment rights." He said the legacy of the case is that "school officials have acquired more and more power over students." Cathy Cowan (formerly Kuhlmeier) agreed when she reflected on the decision in 2001. "I do feel that the legacy of the *Hazelwood* case is one of hurting student First Amendment rights. We should help students, and principals shouldn't be able to control everything," she says. "I think we need to give students room to grow. Students need to be given the chance to do in-depth stories—more than just stories about the soccer game or who was named prom queen."

"I think it's difficult to overstate the damage that the *Hazelwood* decision did to student free expression and press freedom," said Mark Goodman, journalism professor at Kent State and the former head of the Student Press Law Center. To Goodman, *Hazelwood* represented a dramatic departure from the Court's speech-protective standard in *Tinker*. "*Hazelwood* began the downward trend of student First Amendment protection that we are still seeing today."

The *Hazelwood* decision met with outcries from student press advocates, First Amendment purists, and others in the journalism community. Many wondered how school officials could possibly teach young people the value of good journalism if they prevented students from pursing stories about controversial issues.

After the decision, six states passed "anti-*Hazelwood*" laws: Arkansas, Colorado, Iowa, Kansas, Oregon, and Massachusetts (which actually amended its 1974 law). These laws provided greater statutory protection for student speech than the U.S. Supreme Court provided under the First Amendment of the U.S. Constitution. California had already had such a law in place since 1977.

The laws differed in their approach. Some of them simply applied the *Tinker* no-disruptive standard to all student speech. For example, Massachusetts law provides in part: "The right of students to freedom of expression in the public schools of the commonwealth shall not be abridged, provided that such right shall not cause any disruption or disorder within the school." A similar piece of legislation passed in Colorado reads: "If a publication written substantially by students is made generally available throughout a public school, it shall be a public forum for students of such school."

Other laws take a different approach and focus on just student publications. For example, Arkansas's "Student Publications" law provides that such publications receive First Amendment protection unless they are obscene, slanderous, or invasive of privacy rights, incite imminent lawless action, or cause a material or substantial disruption of school activities. Many student speech experts, including Goodman, believe that education remains the most viable way to combat the harmful effects of *Hazelwood*.

HOPE AFTER *HAZELWOOD*?

Hazelwood has created an atmosphere of deference to school officials and a precedent for the censorship of student speech that are controversial. But there remains hope after Hazelwood even beyond the "anti-*Hazelwood*" laws. The lawsuit brought by high school journalist Katy Dean was a bright spot for sure. In 2002, Dean and her colleague Dean Butts, staff members of the *Arrow* at Utica High School in Michigan, learned that a couple living near their school had sued the school district because of bus fumes. Joanne and Rey Frances claimed that diesel fumes from school buses contributed to bad health and constituted a nuisance. Rey later died of lung cancer, and the couple settled their suit with the school district.

Dean interviewed the couple about the lawsuit for several hours. She also attempted to interview school officials but her repeated calls were not returned. Her advisor, Gloria Olman, a national award–winning journalism educator, supported Dean's efforts. "The principal had told the kids the story was a great idea when they had their monthly press conference with him," Olman recalled.

However, the principal had a change of heart after he showed the story to the superintendent's office. School superintendent Joan C. Sergent ordered the principal to pull the story because it involved a matter in litigation. Even though the story dealt with a public lawsuit that had been covered by other newspapers in the community, the school officials censored the article. Olman and the students had to remove the story; they replaced it with an editorial about censorship. Dean was shocked by the censorship: "I couldn't comprehend the possibility that they would censor an article that was factually accurate. It wasn't vulgar or irresponsible in any way. I didn't see it coming."

While she didn't see it coming, school officials may have underestimated Katy Dean. She sued in federal court, contending that her First Amendment rights were violated. "I didn't think it was fair that I could be so easily censored," she said. "It's important that every voice be heard." School officials claimed during litigation that one of the reasons for silencing the students was their use of an unreliable source—*USA Today*. Dean's attorney enlisted the support of experts to give their opinion as to the quality of her journalism. Professor Jane Briggs-Bunting, who had taught journalism at the collegiate level for more than twenty-five years at the time, testified that Dean's story was excellent. "The students did a really good job," Briggs-Bunting reflected in an interview. "Sadly, they did a better job than a lot of reporters at small and large newspapers." In Briggs-Bunting's opinion, "Writing about a public lawsuit should not be controversial."

Federal district court judge Arthur J. Tarnow blasted the school board's decision to pull Dean's article as a blatant example of viewpoint discrimination—silencing the student because her article disagreed with the position of school officials. "The suppression of Dean's article was not reasonable," he wrote. Judge Tarnow then quoted President Dwight D. Eisenhower from a June 1953 speech at Dartmouth College: "Don't join the book burners. Don't think you are going to conceal thoughts by concealing evidence that they ever existed." The school officials thought they could conceal negative information by censoring Dean's article. What they got instead was a civics lesson by a federal judge in *Dean v. Utica Community Schools* (2004).

"We all felt thoroughly vindicated," Olman said. "The [school] district made my work as an adviser extremely difficult after the students filed their lawsuit and the thorough written decision was wonderful, not only for us but also for students nationwide." For her part Katy Dean said that "students must have First Amendment rights, as they are the professional journalists of the future." She had witnessed the fragility of First Amendment freedoms. "I learned that we can never take our civil and personal liberties for granted. They are not guaranteed, as we're often led to believe. America doesn't simply exist as a 'free' nation. Our freedom must constantly be fought for and defended."

CHAPTER 6

BONG HITS

After the 1988 *Hazelwood* decision, the U.S. Supreme Court did not take another pure student free expression case for nearly twenty years. This meant that a trio of First Amendment student speech cases governed American jurisprudence for almost two decades—*Tinker, Fraser,* and *Hazelwood. Hazelwood* applied to school-sponsored student speech. Thus, a student play, many student newspapers (that weren't considered public forums), the school's mascot, or the content of the school's curriculum could be regulated by school officials if they had a legitimate educational, or pedagogical, reason.

Fraser applied to student speech that was considered vulgar, lewd, or plainly offensive. There was disagreement among the lower courts on at least two aspects of *Fraser*. First, lawyers, school officials, and eventually judges disagreed as to whether *Fraser* applied to speech outside the school context or whether it applied only to vulgar and lewd student speech that occurred on school grounds—like Matthew Fraser's speech to the school assembly. The other question was over the reach of the "plainly offensive prong" of *Fraser*.

Some schools applied *Fraser* to any speech they didn't like. In 1997, Nicholas Boroff, a student at Van Wert High School in Ohio, wore a T-shirt picturing the "shock rocker" Marilyn Manson to school. The T-shirt featured a picture of a three-headed Jesus with the words SEE NO TRUTH, HEAR NO TRUTH, SPEAK NO TRUTH. The

back of the shirt featured the word BELIEVE with the letters LIE high-
lighted in red. School officials deemed Boroff's shirt to be offensive
and to promote values counterproductive to the educational environment; they suspended him. Boroff sued in federal court, asserting
his First Amendment rights.

Boroff's attorney, Chris Starkey, contended that school officials could not punish his client for this T-shirt unless they could
show that the shirt was somehow disruptive of school activities. He
also argued that the shirt was no more offensive than other T-shirts
that school officials allowed. Other students had worn "Slayer" and
"MegaDeth" T-shirts without incident. The reason for the censorship, according to Boroff, was what the principal had said to him: the
shirt offended people on religious grounds by mocking Jesus.

Both a federal district court and a federal appeals court rejected
Boroff's lawsuit and ruled in favor of school officials. The U.S. Court
of Appeals for the Sixth Circuit in *Boroff v. Van Wert Board of Education* (2000) determined that school officials could prohibit the
T-shirt under the *Fraser* precedent because the T-shirt was plainly
offensive and promoted disruptive and "demoralizing values."

Other courts also applied a broad reading of *Fraser* and determined that public schools could ban the Confederate flag because
it was a "plainly offensive" symbol. Whatever one thinks of Marilyn
Manson or the Confederate flag, if school officials can prohibit any
student expression they classify as offensive or conveying offensive
ideas, then much student speech is at risk.

Tinker applied to most other student speech that was not school
sponsored (*Hazelwood*) or vulgar or lewd (*Fraser*). There were differences and questions about *Tinker* too. In time, more school board
attorneys interpreted *Tinker* narrowly as a case about viewpoint discrimination, in which school officials violated the First Amendment
because they singled out a particular armband associated with a particular viewpoint. That is one reading of *Tinker*, but not the only
reading. Others read *Tinker* more broadly as protecting a wide swath
of student speech.

Even though there may have been questions of application

about all three decisions, the legal landscape in student speech cases remained relatively stable—at least at the Supreme Court level—for many years. That changed dramatically with "Bong Hits 4 Jesus" and an interesting young man from Juneau, Alaska, named Joseph Frederick.

AN UNUSUAL BANNER

In January 2002, an eighteen-year-old high school senior named Joseph Frederick conducted his ultimate "free speech experiment." When he awoke that day, Frederick knew the Olympic Torch Relay for the upcoming Winter Games was scheduled to pass right across from his high school.

Frederick later said that heavy snowfall that day prevented him from pulling his car out of the driveway and making it to school. Whatever the truth of that statement, Frederick had resolved to proceed with an experiment he had been planning. He had become interested in First Amendment issues during that school year, particularly after he decided to refuse to stand and salute the American flag or to recite the Pledge of Allegiance because he had learned about *West Virginia State Board of Education v. Barnette* (1943). For his act of recalcitrance, a teacher sent Frederick to the assistant principal's office.

Frederick knew that he had a First Amendment right to refuse to stand and recite the Pledge of Allegiance. Justice Robert H. Jackson proclaimed such a right in the famous 1943 flag-salute decision when he wrote: "If there is any fixed star in our constitutional constellation, it is that no official high or petty shall prescribe what shall be orthodox in matters of politics, religion or other matters of public opinion."

That didn't stop school officials from lecturing Frederick about the values of patriotism and love of country. Frederick countered that he loved his country, particularly the Bill of Rights. He believed students should possess First Amendment rights. And he wanted to push the limits.

"I did test the authority of the school administration on numerous occasions," Frederick said in 2009. "I think it's mostly my nature; however I was encouraged even more from things I learned in my elective course American Law. In this course most of the semester was spent on a project where each student was assigned a landmark case and had to research it and present it to the class. Then, we would discuss the meaning of the ruling, and our teacher, Gary Lehnhart, would play devil's advocate in classroom debates with us. I liked asking hypothetical questions a lot."

Frederick was determined to test a hypothetical he had developed concerning students' freedom of speech. So, on that snowy January day in 2002, he waited as the Olympic Torch Relay passed near where he was standing on Glacier Avenue, a public street across from his high school, a spot he had mapped out in advance. Television cameras were there to broadcast the relay, the precursor to one of the most high profile of sporting events.

Frederick, with help from fellow students, unveiled his "free speech experiment"—a fourteen-foot banner featuring a most unusual message spelled out in duct tape for the world to see: BONG HITS 4 JESUS. Frederick said that he had seen the message on a snowboard sticker; a band from New Orleans had that stage name as well. "It was my idea alone to 'do something' during the torch relay," Frederick recalled. "It's hard to say exactly how we made our decision of what to do exactly. My girlfriend and I decided to make a sign of some sort and there were quite a few suggestions from different friends before I finally decided on 'Bong Hits 4 Jesus.'" Whatever the origins of the phrase, Juneau-Douglas High School principal Deborah Morse was less than pleased. She marched across the street and ordered the students to drop the banner. Most quickly complied but Frederick refused. Morse grabbed the banner from Frederick, confiscated it, and ordered him to come to her office. His protestations that his actions were protected by the Bill of Rights and the Constitution fell on deaf ears.

Later that day, Frederick waited to see the principal outside her office. Within a few short hours it was clear that his experiment had produced an unfavorable result. An assistant principal told Frederick that the Bill of Rights did not apply in school—not a good portent for a student waiting to see the principal. Principal Morse then told Frederick that he had violated school policy and had earned himself a five-day suspension. She believed that "Bong Hits 4 Jesus" encouraged illegal drug use—a rampant problem in the public school system. According to Frederick, he responded by quoting the third president of the United States, Thomas Jefferson—"Speech limited is speech lost."

According to Frederick, Morse did not appreciate the reference to Jeffersonian principles and increased Frederick's suspension to ten days. For her part Morse disputed Frederick's account of the Thomas Jefferson quote and the doubling of the suspension. She did acknowledge that Frederick invoked the First Amendment. Whatever the exact nature of the conversation, the scenario set the stage for a legal battle that culminated five years later in *Morse v. Frederick,* a U.S. Supreme Court decision better known as "Bong Hits 4 Jesus."

Unfortunately, Joseph Frederick suffered for his free speech battle and his temerity in tangling with school officials. "The school began to spread rumors that I was a drug addict and drug dealer," he said. "Due to this, some friends' parents forbade their kids from hanging out with me anymore." He claimed that it got much worse than some parents shunning him, however. He said that the local police started viewing him differently. "I started being pulled over twice a day. I would ask the officer, 'Why was I stopped?' and it would always be the same answer: 'You failed to signal when you made a left turn, or didn't come to a complete stop at the stop sign.'"

One day in school, Frederick wore a Leatherman tool that he had been using in auto shop. Though many other teachers and students wore these tools that include small knives, Frederick was treated differently. "The police were called and I was suspended for wearing a Leatherman tool to school. I was using it in auto shop, and over half of the male teachers and students wear them every day despite the fact they include a small knife among the many tools."

Then Frederick was arrested for allegedly trespassing at the city pool. "I was arrested at gunpoint in front of the entire student body and faculty for trespassing," he said. "My car was impounded and torn apart—at least a thousand dollars in damage to the interior. I was released about eight hours later, and the charges dropped since I was clearly not trespassing." Frederick claimed that the police even harassed him one day when he was waiting off school grounds to pick up his girlfriend. "I was parked at the city pool, adjacent to the school, waiting on my girlfriend to get out of class," he recalled. "I was parked under a large sign which read PARKING FOR POOL PATRONS ONLY, NO STUDENT PARKING. I also had a map the school had given me when I was suspended which clearly defined the perimeter of JDHS [Juneau-Douglas High School]. I told the officer, there is a map and instructions on my suspension in the car but he proceeded to hurl me face first into the pavement." Sadly, Joe's father, Frank, also suffered as a result of the free speech battle. "Joe's dad was the risk manager for the insurance company that insured the school district," said Juneau-based attorney Douglas Mertz, who represented the Fredericks in litigation. "The executive director of the company told Frank to get his kid to drop the lawsuit." When Joe did not drop the lawsuit, the company demoted Frank and eventually fired him.

Despite opposition seemingly all over the town, Joseph Frederick did not back down. Instead, he appealed his suspension to the school superintendent, who conducted a hearing. The superintendent, noting that Frederick "has a history of defiant behavior," upheld the suspension but reduced it to eight days.

Frederick then sued in federal court, contending that Morse and the Juneau School Board had violated his First Amendment rights. In May 2003, federal district court judge John W. Sedwick granted summary judgment to the principal. Sedwick first determined that the Olympic relay was a school-sponsored event, glossing over the fact that Joseph Frederick never set foot on campus that day. Sedwick failed to appreciate the fact that there was a good argument that the school had exceeded its authority in disciplining the student. Instead, the judge found that the event unquestionably was a school-sponsored event. The judge noted that Morse allowed the band and the cheerleaders to take time off to participate in the rally.

She also authorized teachers to take their classes to the relay to watch the historic event.

Judge Sedwick reasoned that Morse could punish Frederick under the *Fraser* standard for his "plainly offensive" speech. He added that "Frederick's expression directly conflicted with the school's deterrence of illegal drug use and addiction."

Sedwick said that even if the principal had violated Frederick's First Amendment rights, she was entitled to qualified immunity. This doctrine provides that government officials are not liable for damages resulting from legal violations if they do not violate clearly established constitutional or statutory law. In other words, if a court classifies an area of law as sufficiently muddled, government officials—such as school administrators—can violate the law with no monetary penalties because the state of the law is less than clear. The doctrine of qualified immunity is a boon for school officials who admittedly sometimes operate in gray areas of legal uncertainty.

Frederick then appealed to the U.S. Court of Appeals for the Ninth Circuit, which reversed Sedwick's ruling in March 2006 in *Frederick v. Morse*. For the first time, Joseph Frederick and his attorney, Douglas Mertz, had a bit of good fortune.

At the circuit appeals courts—the intermediate courts in the federal judicial system—cases are usually heard by panels of three judges. Attorneys talk about getting a "good panel or a bad panel." Mertz got a good panel in that he drew a federal judge from Alaska named Andrew Kleinfeld. Several years earlier Kleinfeld wrote a very strong dissenting opinion in a student speech case called *Lavine v. Blaine School District* (2002), in which a student was punished for writing a poem about school violence. In his written opinion in *Lavine*, Kleinfeld demonstrated an extraordinary knowledge of legal precedent in the area of student speech and strong sensitivity to student speech rights. He did not disappoint in Joseph Frederick's case.

Writing for a unanimous three-judge panel, Kleinfeld reasoned that Frederick's claim was controlled not by *Fraser*, but by the seminal *Tinker* decision. Applying *Tinker*, Kleinfeld reasoned that Morse failed to show "a reasonable concern about the likelihood of substantial disruption." School attorneys pressed hard for the application of *Fraser*, reasoning that student speech about bong hits is "plainly offensive." However, Kleinfeld noted that Matthew Fraser spoke about sex before a school assembly. Instead, Joseph Frederick spoke about marijuana usage in a state that has had a serious political debate about the legalization of marijuana. The school board attorneys argued that *Fraser* stands for the principle that the school can prevent any speech that is inconsistent with the school's educational mission. Kleinfeld rejected this broad analysis with incisive examples.

> All sorts of missions are undermined by legitimate and protected speech—a school's anti-gun mission would be undermined by a student passing around copies of John R. Lott's book, *More Guns, Less Crime*; a school's anti-alcohol mission would be undermined by a student e-mailing links to a medical study showing less heart disease among moderate drinkers than teetotalers; and a school's traffic safety mission would be undermined by a student circulating copies of articles showing that traffic cameras and automatic ticketing systems for cars that run red lights increase accidents.

To Kleinfeld, it was clear that the proper analysis was whether or not Frederick's speech had created a disruption. He quoted the school district's response as to how the "Bong Hits 4 Jesus" banner caused a disruption.

> Display of the banner would be construed by many, including students, district personnel, parents and others witnessing the display of the banner, as advocating or promoting illegal drug use which is inconsistent with the district's basic educational mission to promote a healthy, drug-free life style. Failure to react to the display would appear to give the district's imprimatur to that message and would be inconsistent with the district's responsibility to teach students the boundaries of socially appropriate behavior.

Significant to Judge Kleinfeld was the fact that school officials had failed to mention how the banner disrupted anything that happened in school classrooms. "No educational function was disrupted by the banner displayed during the Coca-Cola sponsored Olympics event," he determined.

Kleinfeld then ruled that Morse was not entitled to qualified immunity, because *Tinker* "is so clear and well-settled that no reasonable government official could have believed the censorship and punishment of Frederick's speech to be lawful." It was a resounding victory for Joseph Frederick, but would it last?

SUPREME CONFLICT

The U.S. Supreme Court surprised some observers by taking the case from the school district's appeal. Battle lines were drawn: on one side was former independent counsel and federal appeals court judge Ken Starr representing the school district pro bono (for free); the American Civil Liberties Union, through cooperating attorney Mertz, ably represented Frederick. Many groups lined up in support of Joseph Frederick, including several conservative groups normally associated with the protection of conservative political and religious speech. Groups such as the Alliance Defense Fund and Liberty Legal rallied to Joseph Frederick's cause even though they in no way condoned his peculiar message. "There were some strange bedfellows in the case," Mertz recalled. "You don't ordinarily see the ACLU and the conservative religious think tanks agreeing and taking the same position in a case." So why was Frederick's case attracting such a unique coalition?

The school district had advanced the argument that—under the precedent set by the Matthew Fraser case—Principal Morse could ban any type of speech that was "plainly offensive" or that advocated any cause that was antithetical to the school's mission. Many conservative groups rightly saw this as the possible death knell for much conservative student speech if schools adopted such a rule. In their view, student speech about the evils of abortion, for example, could be censored under Principal Morse's reasoning. So too might religious expression against same-sex marriage. So, Joseph Frederick had some unlikely allies in his legal fight.

The case came before the Court in March 2007, with Starr leading off the oral arguments, as he was representing the appellants—the parties appealing the lower-court decision. "Illegal drugs and the glorification of the drug culture are profoundly serious problems for our nation," Starr began. After some tough questioning from Justice David Souter, Starr insisted that "this case is ultimately about drugs and other illegal substances." Justice Ruth Bader Ginsburg then asked whether there would have been a problem if Frederick's banner had read "Bong Stinks 4 Jesus."

Chief Justice John G. Roberts Jr. followed with a probing question that seemed to indicate he was worried about the argument that school officials could prohibit any speech they deemed offensive or contrary to the educational mission of the school. "Now, do they get to dictate the content of speech on all of those issues simply because they have adopted that as part of their educational mission?" Starr never managed a complete answer, as Justice Ginsburg intervened with yet another question. But Starr perhaps saw the writing on the wall that he might not prevail with his broadest arguments so he shrewdly returned to the drug theme. "What is happening here of course in this case, it can be decided very narrowly, that drugs, alcohol and tobacco just have no place in the schools," he said.

Deputy Solicitor General Edwin Kneedler, an experienced advocate before the high court, then spoke on behalf of the United States as an amicus in the case. Kneedler also stressed that this case concerned speech about drugs. He reminded the Court that it had found that drug use was a serious issue in schools in an earlier opinion, *Board of Education v. Earls* (2001), in which the Court had approved random drug testing for students taking part in extracurricular activities.

Mertz then stepped to the podium and immediately faced questions about qualified immunity—about whether it was clearly established that Principal Morse had violated the First Amendment in punishing Frederick for his unusual banner. It did not look good for Joseph Frederick on the qualified immunity issue when Justice Souter—who had shown a proclivity for protecting speech in his tenure on the Court—also seemed concerned about whether the law was clearly established: "We've been debating this in this courtroom for going on an hour, and it seems to me however you come out, there is reasonable debate. Should the teacher have known, even in the . . . calm deliberative atmosphere of the school later, what the correct answer is?" Mertz responded well: "We believe at the very least she should have known that one cannot punish a nondisruptive holding of a sign because it said something you disagreed with."

DECISION TIME

In June 2007, the Supreme Court sided with Principal Morse and the school district. Chief Justice Roberts wrote the Court's majority opinion that created a pro-drug-speech exception to *Tinker*. He determined at the outset that this was a school speech case and that Morse had jurisdiction and authority to regulate student speech at a "school-sanctioned" event. Roberts acknowledged that "there is some uncertainty at the outer boundaries as to when courts should apply school-speech precedents," but not in this case.

"We conclude that the school officials in this case did not violate the First Amendment by confiscating the pro-drug banner and suspending the student responsible for it," Roberts wrote. All nine justices agreed that Principal Morse was entitled to qualified immunity. However, the Court split much more closely on the underlying First Amendment question.

Roberts concluded that school officials can censor student speech that they reasonably believe advocates illegal drug use. Even though the legalization of marijuana is an important public policy issue in the United States, the Court cited prior precedent favoring the principal's argument that students simply don't possess the same level of constitutional rights as adults do to discuss such issues in school.

Roberts did provide a golden nugget for student rights advocates—one that went unnoticed by many. He rejected Ken Starr's broad argument that the school could prohibit the banner because it constituted "plainly offensive" speech. "Petitioners urge us to adopt the broader rule that Frederick's speech is proscribable because it is plainly 'offensive'" as that term is used in *Fraser*," he wrote. "We think this stretches Fraser too far; that case should not be read to encompass any speech that could fit under some definition of 'offensive.' After all, much political and religious speech might be perceived as offensive to some. The concern here is not that Frederick's speech was offensive, but that it was reasonably viewed as promoting illegal drug use." Perhaps Roberts was persuaded on that one point by the amicus briefs filed by the various religious liberty groups.

Justice Samuel Alito, joined by Anthony Kennedy, wrote a concurring opinion emphasizing that principals can punish only speech that is reasonably believed to be advocating illegal drug use and not political speech about important issues, including the legalization of marijuana. Alito's opinion seems to suggest that he would have ruled differently if Frederick's banner had instead read "Legalize Marijuana." Alito stressed that he rejected Starr's argument that school administrators can restrict any student speech that is contrary to the educational mission of the school. "The opinion of the Court does not endorse the broad argument advanced by petitioners and the United States that the First Amendment permits public school officials to censor any student speech that interferes with a school's 'educational mission,'" he wrote. "This argument can easily be manipulated in dangerous ways, and I would reject it before such abuse occurs."

Justice Clarence Thomas concurred with an opinion calling for the overruling of *Tinker*, writing that it "is without basis in the Constitution."

Thomas also warned about the uncertainty in student speech jurisprudence. "I am afraid that our jurisprudence now says that students have a right to speak in schools except when they don't—a standard continuously developed through litigation against local schools and their administrators," he wrote. "In my view, petitioners could prevail for a much simpler reason: As originally understood, the Constitution does not afford students a right to free speech in public schools."

He also hearkened back to Justice Hugo Black's famous dissent in *Tinker* when he warned about creating a revolutionary era of permissiveness. Thomas wrote that Black's dissent has "proved prophetic."

Justice Stephen Breyer wrote that he believed the Court should simply decide the case on qualified-immunity grounds and not wade into the deeper First Amendment waters. Justice John Paul Stevens authored a dissent in which he took the majority to task on the underlying First Amendment ruling. "In my judgment, the First Amendment protects student speech if the message itself neither violates a permissible rule nor expressly advocates conduct that is illegal and harmful to students," he wrote. "This nonsense banner does neither, and the Court does serious violence to the First Amendment in upholding—indeed, lauding—a school's decision to punish Frederick for expressing a view with which it disagreed."

Joseph Frederick was understandably upset by the Court's decision. "It was the final straw that caused me to lose all faith in the American judicial system. It was extremely sad, because I found out that many of the things I had learned in Mr. Lehnhart's classes weren't necessarily true. I had thought that the justices were supposed to go by previous Supreme Court rulings and by the Bill of Rights."

Fellow former Supreme Court litigant John Tinker agreed with Frederick's assessment. "I do have a problem with the *Morse v. Frederick* decision," he said. "Finding out that Americans don't really have a right to free speech was like a child finally learning that Santa Claus is merely a myth."

Frederick's case did not end at the Supreme Court. There were remaining state law claims that Mertz had advocated on behalf of Frederick. "The case was settled by December 2008," Mertz said. "All the claims were dismissed and all records of discipline wiped away and they agreed to pay Joe about $45,000. As part of the settlement, they also agreed that they would hold a forum at the school moderated by a neutral observer where we could present our side of the case."

Joseph Frederick recalled the forum as well. "The only real grati-
fying part of it was seeing the disgusted expressions of my previous
archenemies."

The events on January 24, 2002, had ramifications far beyond
Juneau and even beyond the Marble Palace, as the Supreme Court is
commonly called. Joseph Frederick's free speech experiment gave the
nation a rare and rich opportunity to discuss the free speech rights
of public school students, the power of school officials to enforce
discipline and ensure safety, and the meaning of those first forty-five
words of the Bill of Rights.

The seemingly nonsensical message "Bong Hits 4 Jesus" led to a
renewed discussion about how to calibrate the delicate balance between a safe learning environment and a fostering of students' individual rights. As Starr wrote in a 2008 law review article on the
case for the *University of California-Davis Law Review*, "Even with its
whimsical facts, the so-called Bong Hits 4 Jesus case has provided a
serious occasion to consider afresh the frequently recurring highly
practical issue of student speech in schools."

"*Morse v. Frederick* stands for two things," said Mertz. "On the
positive side, the Court rejected the school district's argument that
you can suppress any student speech that is inconsistent with the
school's educational mission and it retained the *Tinker* holding. On
the negative side, the Court's decision showed a continued willingness to carve out more exceptions to *Tinker*. It was particularly
troubling that the Court appeared to be willing to defer to school
officials' judgment that this was pro-drug speech."

It's clear that *Morse* gives school officials the power to silence
student speech that promotes illegal drug use. But does the rationale
of the high court decision apply to any student speech that appears
to promote any unlawful action? Does it apply to any student speech
that threatens the safety of students?

Some courts seemingly have interpreted *Morse* as a pro-drug-
speech exception to *Tinker*. However, at least one lower court, the
Fifth Circuit in *Ponce v. Socorro Independent School District* (2007),
applied *Morse*—and specifically Justice Samuel Alito's concurring

opinion—to find that school officials can restrict student speech that they reasonably believe poses a danger to school safety. First Amendment commentator Douglas Lee pointed out in a column that this decision "extended *Morse* to allow school administrators to apply zero-tolerance rules to threats of violence and potentially other subjects of student speech."

Though it likely will take years to determine whether student speech rights went up in smoke during Joseph Frederick's case, the decision certainly gave school officials another justification for limiting certain types of student speech.

CHAPTER 7

COLUMBINE

In February 1999, a high school student penned an essay for his creative writing class about a mysterious man with black gloves, a black trench coat, and a black duffel bag who massacred a group of students he disdainfully referred to as "preps":

> Before I could see a reaction from the preps, the man had dropped his duffel bag, and pulled out one of the pistols with his left hand. Three shots were fired. Three shots hit the largest prep in the head. The shining of the streetlights caused a visible reaction off of the droplets of blood as they flew away from the skull. The blood spatters showered the preps buddies, as they were to [sic] paralyzed to run.

The violent essay included students falling helplessly and terrorized victims. The piece lacked any empathy whatsoever for the tortured victims—only for the murderous hero-villain. The antihero caused carnage with guns, a black knife, and an explosive device. At the end of his rampage, the man turned to glare at the writer with an "unforgettable look."

"If I could face an emotion of god, it would have looked like the man," the student writer continued. "I not only saw in his face, but also felt eminating [sic] from him power, complacence, closure and godliness." The student wrote that he "understood" the actions of the man who was hell bent on unleashing death and destruction. The student's essay conveyed a protagonist prone to acting out his selfish desires—no matter how harmful—in the spirit of Fyodor Dostoyevsky's "superman" character from *Crime and Punishment*, Raskolnikov.

The student turned the essay in to his creative writing teacher, Judith Kelly, who recognized the creativity and storytelling gifts of her young pupil. She also saw something more sinister—a disturbed and troubled soul. She noted the "great details" and scribbled "quite an ending" on the assignment. But, she also was perturbed by the student's excessive use of profanity in the piece, writing: "You are an excellent writer and storyteller, but I have some problems with this one."

Kelly found the piece to be a glorification of violence, an over-the-top homage to a homicidal maniac. In an official police statement, she would later describe the essay as "literary and ghastly—the most vicious story I ever read." After reading the assignment, Kelly questioned her student about his seeming preoccupation with murder and mayhem, with a character who seemed to enjoy the visceral thrill of the kill.

The student assured her that the essay was simply fiction, an outlet for his imagination. The teacher didn't buy that explanation, perhaps in part because the teenager earlier in the semester had turned in a twelve-page report on the "Mind and Motives of Charles Manson." Upon reading the violent essay, Kelly spoke with the student's parents, who assured her it was probably all attributable to adolescent angst. It was—after all—merely a literary exercise, not a psychological profile.

Despite assurances from the teenager's parents, Kelly contacted a school guidance counselor, who spoke to the boy. Once again the student said, "It's just a story."

It turned out that it was more than "just a story." The story's author was seventeen-year-old Dylan Klebold, a senior at Columbine High School in Littleton, Colorado. Klebold and his friend Eric

Harris—another creative writing student—carried out the notorious shooting at their school on April 20, 1999, that left thirteen dead and many others wounded. The Columbine shooting not only changed the culture in America's schools but also left indelible imprints on the future of student speech.

COPYCAT

Klebold and Harris's attack inspired a lonely eighth-grader in Virginia named Seung-Hui Cho, who later said in his writings and rantings that he identified with the two Columbine shooters. He wrote that he wanted to carry out "another Columbine."

Cho, whose family had moved to the United States from South Korea when he was eight, managed to graduate from high school and enter Virginia Tech University despite growing up with selective mutism. Behind the young man's silent exterior, anxiety and anger were hardening into rage. Cho routinely gave one-word responses to queries from other students, even his dorm roommates. Once he signed a class roll with a question mark, causing the professor to ask if he should call him "Mr. Question Mark." Cho told one of his teachers that he wanted to write poetry. It was in his creative writing classes that Cho offered a glimpse of his tortured soul. A one-act play he turned in for class titled *Richard McBeef* dealt with a stepson's fantasies of killing his pedophilic stepfather only to suffer death at the hands of the demented stepfather. "Out of sheer desecrated hurt and anger, Richard lifts his large arms and swings a deadly blow at the thirteen year old boy," the last line of the play reads. The play caused several of his classmates to wonder about their strangely silent classmate. One of Cho's college classmates, Ian MacFarlane, later blogged for AOL: "When we read Cho's plays, it was like something out of a nightmare. The plays had really twisted, macabre violence that used weapons I wouldn't have even thought of. . . . We students were talking to each other with serious worry about whether he could be a school shooter. I was even thinking of scenarios of what I would do in case he did come in with a gun. I was that freaked out about him."

In 2005, professor and famed poet Nikki Giovanni went to English department chair Lucinda Roy with serious concerns about Cho. According to later accounts, the disturbed young man had written a poem that she and her class found frightening. Giovanni asserted that she wanted Cho removed from the class. Roy ended up having to conduct one-on-one tutoring sessions with the boy, who showed up in sunglasses and responded with disconcerting delays before finally speaking slowly. Cho exhibited such alarming warning signs of potential violence that police escorted him off campus at one point after a roommate reported a suicide threat. A county magistrate found probable cause that Cho was "mentally ill" and an "imminent danger." He was kept overnight in a mental hospital but later released. Cho did not receive continued mental health care but later was able to buy guns despite the magistrate's earlier finding.

Cho should have received mental health care. On April 16, 2007—nearly eight years to the day after the Columbine shooting—the twenty-three-year-old Cho shot and killed thirty-two students and faculty members at Virginia Tech before killing himself. As with the Columbine shooters, Cho's violent-themed writings in school provided insight into his psyche. Roy writes in her memoir *No Right to Remain Silent*: "But it is dangerous to assume that all those who produce writing that contains violence are themselves potential perpetrators of violence. If we believe that, we would have to incarcerate everyone from Stephen King to the Coen brothers, along with the writers of *The Sopranos*, *Deadwood*, and *CSI*, to name just a few."

It's an important point, yet one that's part of a complicated broader argument when one considers the violent creative writing that preceded the killings at Columbine and Virginia Tech. Many of our most highly regarded cultural works portray violence, from William Shakespeare to Bret Easton Ellis. In an essay for *Entertainment Weekly*, "On Predicting Violence," best-selling author Stephen King reflected candidly that some of the early writing he did in school "would have raised red flags." He said that for most creative writers "the imagination serves as an excretory channel for violence: We visualize what we will never actually do." There are exceptions, of course—as King writes of Cho: "Dude was crazy."

CHANGE IN STUDENT SPEECH

Columbine had an impact beyond Seung-Hui Cho and other copy-cat shooters. It changed the mindset of school officials across the country, who viewed students differently and clamped down on a wide array of unusual student expression. Author and journalist Jon Katz referred to the phenomenon as the "silencing of the weird."

In America's post-Columbine school system, a "zero tolerance" policy, traditionally reserved for drugs and weapons, spread to include controversial student speech. After the school shootings, students were punished for dark poetry, rap songs, Halloween essays, doodles of teachers and students with sticks in their heads, and other violent-themed expression. Fear of another Columbine led to some gross overreactions with students suspended, expelled, sent to psychologists, and even jailed for relatively minor offenses or for harmless creative expression.

The Columbine shootings understandably heightened school officials' concerns about ensuring a safe learning environment for their students. While no one questions that school officials have an interest in and responsibility for ensuring school safety, it's also obvious that the quest for safety can lead to the trampling of student free expression rights. In the age of zero tolerance, some students became victims of Columbine in another sense. "We are in a new paradigm of lockdown and surveillance," says John Whitehead, founder of the Rutherford Institute, a civil liberties group based in Virginia.

A prime example of the "new paradigm" was the increasing number of school officials who adopted a zero-tolerance mindset regarding any violent-themed student work—even creative writing, which often explores taboo subjects. The results were often wildly and unjustifiably punitive. Five months after Columbine, in October 1999, a middle school student in Texas spent several days in jail for a violent-themed Halloween essay for which he received an A from his teacher. Three months after that, in January 2000, a high school honors student in Kansas was expelled for writing a poem about seeking revenge against someone for killing her dog. In March 2001, a student in Louisiana with no history of violence was punished for a drawing he had created at home two years earlier that showed his school under attack. Even more outrageous, the student never brought the drawing to school—his younger brother brought the art pad to school to show his own picture, not knowing that his sibling's old picture was also in there.

After Columbine, violent-themed student works suddenly qualified as "true threats."

TRUE THREATS

The U.S. Supreme Court created the true-threat exception in First Amendment jurisprudence in the same year (1969) as the famous *Tinker* decision. In *Watts v. United States*, the Court determined that the young African American Vietnam War protestor Robert Paul Watts did not utter a true threat when he allegedly said to another person at a war protest: "If they ever make me carry a rifle, the first man I want in my sights is L. B. J. [President Lyndon B. Johnson]" For this, government officials charged Watts with violating a federal law prohibiting threats against the president. Fortunately, the Court determined that Watts's rhetoric was mere "political hyperbole," not a true threat—and was therefore protected by the First Amendment. Unfortunately, the Court did not articulate a definition for a true threat.

Such uncertainty from the high court often leads to confusion in the lower courts—and uncertainty for litigants. In setting out their "true threat" standard, some of these courts focus on the probable reaction by a reasonable recipient of the statement: Would that person perceive a true threat? Others focus on how a reasonable speaker should foresee that others would take her statements: Should she foresee her statements will be perceived as a true threat?

Some courts have used a complex multifactor "true threat" test in the schools, under which school officials should focus on factors including (1) the reaction of the listener and other recipients; (2) whether the threat was conditional; (3) whether the speaker communicated the statement(s) directly to the recipient; (4) whether the speaker had a history of making threats; (5) whether the recipient knew the speaker had a propensity for violence. The multifactor test—one that speaks of "totality of the circumstances"—often justifies school officials' action. In a post-Columbine world, courts have created very flexible definitions of true threats in the school context. How else can one explain what happened to Texas seventh-grader Christopher Beamon? In October 1999, his teacher asked her students to write a creative Halloween piece, an assignment the thirteen-year-old tackled with relish. The Ponder, Texas, native wrote a story that his English teacher, Amanda Henry, awarded an A, with extra credit for reading it out loud to his classmates. The piece featured kids with their heads cut off and Mrs. Henry accidentally shot.

Though his teacher loved Christopher's essay, other students told their parents, who then called the principal to express their concerns. Adding to the mounting concern was Beamon's disciplinary history—something that can follow a student around like a scarlet letter. Even though Beamon had no history of violence, some parents told the school principal that they feared the student would harm their children. Principal Chance Allen then called the police, who transported Beamon to a juvenile detention facility. Juvenile court judge Darlene Whitten ordered Beamon to be held for ten days as a "delinquent"—the juvenile court mantra for an incorrigible youth incapable of adhering to laws. "Schools are like airports in that even jokes there should be taken seriously," Whitten said. Of Beamon's prior disciplinary incidents on his school record, his attorney later said that the most serious was "horseplay in the hallways."

He spent six days in detention. The school superintendent, Bryon Welch, later said, "we are concerned with the safety and security of everyone, and the balance point is, when someone feels threatened, we had to step in and do something." They did something—they incarcerated a boy for a piece of creative writing.

Dallas-based attorney William B. Short Jr. decided to represent Beamon, even though it was far from his normal practice of law. Short's wife had worked with Christopher Beamon's mother, and Short considered the case an outrageous overreaction on the part of school officials. A barrage of national and even international media attention descended upon officials in Ponder, Texas.

"I was supposed to write a horror story," Beamon said. "I don't think I did anything wrong." Neither did many in the national media, including the *New York Times* and other major news outlets. District attorney Bruce Isaacks declined to prosecute, noting: "It looks to me the child was doing what the teacher told him to do, which was write a scary story." Much to his mother's relief, Whitten released Beamon after six days. But the chilling effect of such an ordeal imposed an arctic freeze upon student creative writing. The actions of the principal, superintendent, and juvenile judge earned them the dubious distinction of a Jefferson Muzzle award from a civil liberties group, the Thomas Jefferson Center for the Protection of Free Expression, in 2000. It also inspired a healthy dose of media criticism. Chicago journalist John Kass expressed it well in his editorial "Fear of Violence Getting Best of Common Sense." Columnist Joseph Farrah wrote: "How can anyone, let alone a 13-year-old kid working on a school assignment, be locked up for writing anything in the land of the First Amendment?" The easy answer was Columbine and the looming fear of another school shooting.

THE CASE OF THE STOLEN POEM

Beamon wasn't alone in suffering at the hands of overzealous school officials. In Pulaski County, Arkansas, an eighth-grader known in court papers by his initials "J. M." wrote a poem-letter about his former girlfriend, who had broken up with him during the summer of 2000. J. M.'s favorite artist was Marshall Mathers—better known to the world as Eminem—a multiplatinum, mega–best-selling phenom known for his clever lyrics and wordplay, often peppered with obscenities and violent language.

Emulating his musical hero, J. M. created two "rap songs" in which he fantasized about raping, sodomizing, and murdering his girlfriend. He repeatedly referred to his former girlfriend as "bitch," "whore," "slut," and worse. At the same time he was writing these poems, J. M. was known in his community as a fourteen-year-old boy who had earned a certificate from the local Chamber of Commerce and had a good school record.

J. M. never showed his signed letters or "songs" to his girlfriend. Instead, he kept them in a lockbox in his bedroom at home. It was only after a friend of J. M.'s found and stole the papers and gave them to J. M.'s ex-girlfriend—all without J. M.'s knowledge—that others learned about the young man's dark writing. Scared and sickened by what she read, J. M.'s former girlfriend turned the poems over to a school resource officer and school officials reacted swiftly. The principal believed that J. M. had issued a terroristic threat to another student—an offense punishable by expulsion in the student code of conduct. The school board upheld the principal's recommendation and expelled J. M.

Through his parents, J. M. sued, claiming a violation of his First Amendment free speech rights and his rights to due process under the Fourteenth Amendment. Initially, J. M. found the federal courts a friendlier forum than school, as a federal trial court judge ruled that school officials violated his constitutional rights. Initially, a three-judge panel of the federal appeals court agreed with, or affirmed, the lower court decision. However, the school board appealed to the full panel of judges on the Eighth Circuit, an en banc review.

The full Eighth Circuit adopted and walked through its own malleable test for determining if student speech constitutes a true threat. The court focused on the reaction of the girlfriend to the letter, rather than whether J. M. actually intended to give her the letter.

"The fact that J. M. did not personally deliver the letter to [his ex-girlfriend] did not dispel its threatening nature," the court majority wrote. Instead the majority focused on the horrid content of the letter and its preoccupation with violence, concluding that a "reasonable recipient" of such a letter might perceive it as a real threat.

Four judges dissented. They accused the majority of creating a "dangerously broad precedent by holding that any private utterance of an intent to injure another person is not entitled to First Amendment protection." The dissenting judges added that J. M. created the letters in the privacy of his own home and never intended to take them to school. It was only through the act of theft by his supposed "friend" that one of the letters ever made it onto school grounds. The letters were akin to a private diary, they argued, not intended to be opened and read by others.

"The record demonstrates that, regrettably, J.M. thought Eminem's lyrics were the best source of inspiration for his catharsis," the dissent wrote. "The shocking contents of the letter alone, however, do not warrant the finding of a true threat."

"LAST WORDS"

One of the most troubling facets of these student speech cases is the fact that even if a court determines that a student did not utter a true threat in violent-themed writing, it does not mean that the student will prevail. A high school student in Blaine, Washington, learned this firsthand in October 1998.

James Lavine wrote a poem entitled "Last Words" that depicted the troubled mindset of a student who killed his classmates and teachers. Lavine claimed he wrote the poem to "understand the phenomenon" of school shootings, such as the one that happened in nearby Springfield, Oregon, in May 1998. In that shooting, fifteen-year-old Kip Kinkel killed his parents and then killed two students at his high school.

The poem read:

As each day passed,
I watched,
Love sprout, from the most,
Unlikely places,
Wich reminds,
Me that,
Beauty is in the eye's,

. . .

I pulled my gun,
From its case,
And began to load it.
I remember,
Thinking at least I won't,

Go alone,
As I,
Jumped in,
The car,
All I could think about,
Was I would not,
Go alone,
As I walked,
Through the empty halls,
I could feel,
My hart pounding,
As I approached,
The classroom door,
I drew my gun and,
Threw open the door,
Bang, Bang, Bang-Bang.
When it was all over,
28 were,
dead.

Lavine showed the poem to his mother, who urged him not to take it to school. She warned him that school officials could misinterpret the poem and overreact—a wise premonition that proved the adage "Listen to your mother." He ignored his mother's advice. Instead he took the work to school and showed it to his English teacher, Vivian Bleeker. Lavine turned in a couple assignments and then his poem, which was not an assignment. The poem alarmed Bleeker, who thought that Lavine might harm himself. She showed the poem to a school counselor who also expressed concern, partly because two years earlier James Lavine had confided to her that he had harbored suicidal thoughts. The counselor also knew he had been involved in a domestic disturbance with his father and had recently broken up with his girlfriend. The chain reaction continued, as the counselor showed the poem to the vice principal, who then contacted the police department.

Law enforcement went to the Lavine home to evaluate the teenager. A deputy sheriff interviewed him and reported his findings to the state psychiatrist, who decided there was no need to confine the student involuntarily. The principal, however, decided to "emergency expel" Lavine until he was evaluated directly by a mental health professional. The principal wrote a letter to Lavine's parents saying their son had written a poem "which implied extreme violence to our student body."

A different school psychologist next examined the student. After three sessions, this psychologist concluded that Lavine was not a danger to himself or others. School officials allowed him to return to school. He had missed seventeen days. Lavine and his father then sued the school in federal court, contending that the school had violated the student's First Amendment rights.

U.S. district judge Barbara Jacobs Rothstein ruled in the student's favor, determining that the school's actions were not justified. She noted that school officials had a "compelling interest in ensuring the safety of the students and staff," but reasoned that they overreacted based on the content of the poem. Rothstein wrote that the poem could not reasonably be construed as a true threat, as "there was no overt action, violent demeanor, or other threatening behavior manifested by James Lavine."

In a footnote, Rothstein took a swipe at school officials' justification, the claim that they were concerned about the possibly fragile mental state of James Lavine: "Suicidal ideation is a far cry from threatened violence and is hardly uncommon among teen-aged persons. Anyone truly concerned with James Lavine's mental health should have known that emergency expulsion of such a student would not be constructive." She also criticized school officials for imposing excessive punishment: "A temporary suspension pending psychiatric examination would have been a far less drastic measure and ultimately would have accomplished the defendants' purpose."

School authorities then appealed to a three-judge panel of the U.S. Court of Appeals for the Ninth Circuit, an appeals court often considered to the political left of most of the American judiciary.

Recall that the Ninth Circuit had ruled in favor of Matthew Fraser and Joseph Frederick in their cases before those student litigants lost in the U.S. Supreme Court. A panel of the Ninth Circuit also had caused a national outrage in its 2002 ruling, widely perceived as a politically liberal decision, that the 1954 addition to the Pledge of Allegiance of the words "under God"—to distinguish us from the "godless Communists"—violated the Establishment Clause.

Despite some famously liberal decisions, the Ninth Circuit is also a very large circuit, with judges whose rulings reflect a wide range of professional and personal ideologies. James Lavine drew a less-than-ideal three-judge panel that analyzed the case far differently than Judge Rothstein had.

The panel ruled in 2001 that under *Tinker,* the school officials could reasonably forecast that Lavine's poem would constitute a substantial disruption. The appeals court determined that an application of the *Tinker* standard required a court to examine the totality of the circumstances. To the court, there were a number of facts in the *Lavine* case—when considered together—that justified the officials' harsh punishment. These facts included the student's previous conversations with the school counselor about suicidal thoughts; a domestic dispute between Lavine and his father; his recent breakup with his girlfriend; and past disciplinary incidents. The court also bluntly stated that it relied on the content of the poem: "'Last Words' is filled with imagery of violent death and suicide. Even in its most mild interpretation, the poem appears to be a 'cry for help' from a troubled teenager contemplating suicide."

The Ninth Circuit—which decided the case two years after Columbine—emphasized that the case had to be interpreted against "the backdrop of actual school shootings" and concluded that school officials met the *Tinker* standard because they had a reasonable forecast of substantial disruption—"that James Lavine was intending to inflict injury upon himself or others."

The appeals court acknowledged that the student's mother may have been prescient in saying that school officials would overreact, but the appeals court said it must accord deference to school officials on safety issues. "School officials have a difficult task in balancing safety concerns against chilling free expression," the Ninth Circuit wrote in *Lavine v. Blaine School District* (2001). "This case demonstrates how difficult that task can be."

Lavine petitioned the Ninth Circuit for en banc review. Although the Ninth Circuit denied review, three judges dissented. Andrew Kleinfeld—the Alaskan nominated to the bench by President George H.W. Bush who later defended the free speech rights of Joseph Frederick in "Bong Hits 4 Jesus"—said the majority had distorted the principles of *Tinker:*

> After today, members of the black trench coat clique in high schools in the western United States will have to hide their art work. They have lost their free speech rights. If a teacher, administrator, or student finds their art disturbing, they can be punished, even though they say nothing disruptive, defamatory or indecent and do not intend to threaten or harm anyone. School officials may now subordinate students' freedom of expression to a policy of making high schools cozy places, like daycare centers, where no one may be made uncomfortable by the knowledge that others have dark thoughts, and all the art is of hearts and smiley faces. The court has adopted a new doctrine in First Amendment law, that high school students may be punished for non-threatening speech that administrators believe may indicate that the speaker is emotionally disturbed and therefore dangerous.

Judge Kleinfeld wrote that the panel had created new law at James Lavine's expense by formulating a "new First Amendment rule" that allowed school officials to punish students for nondisruptive speech simply because officials have a concern that the students "might be dangerous to themselves or others." According to Kleinfeld, the majority's decision turns a public high school into a "constitutional black hole, where freedom of speech exists only to the extent that administrators are comfortable with it." He added that the school district's actions, instead of making school safer, could actually make it more unsafe, writing "suppression of speech may reduce security as well as liberty. Allowing the school to punish a student for writing a poem about a school killer may foster school killings, by drying up information from students about their own and other students' emotional troubles. If the students don't talk, the administrators and medical professionals won't find out about problems that speech might reveal."

ZERO TOLERANCE RUN AMOK

If James Lavine thought he had it bad, perhaps he needed to talk to Louisiana student Adam Porter, whose ordeal brings to mind the old saying that "truth is stranger than fiction." The Louisiana teen was expelled from school, charged with two felonies, and thrown in jail for four days for a two-year-old drawing that his younger brother inadvertently brought to school.

In 1999, fourteen-year-old Porter made a drawing of his school, East Ascension High, under attack by a missile launcher, armed individuals, and explosives. The drawing also contained disparaging remarks about his principal and a racial epithet.

Porter showed the drawing to his mother, Mary LeBlanc. "I remember when Adam sketched the drawing in his bedroom," she said. "I asked him what he was doing and he said he was 'just playing.' I found it humorous, not a serious thing. I talked with him about it. He had no violent intent at all when he made the drawing. In fact, I forgot about it until two years later."

The sketch pad was thrown into a closet, where it remained for two years until Porter's younger brother, Andrew Breen, discovered it in March 2001. Breen drew a picture of an animal in it and then took the pad on the school bus to show one of his teachers. On the bus, Breen showed his drawing to a fellow student. Flipping through the pad, that student noticed Porter's two-year-old drawing. Alarmed, the student told the school bus driver.

Breen received a three-day suspension for bringing an inappropriate drawing to Galvez Middle School. Meanwhile, officials were contacted at the high school and informed of Porter's drawing.

School officials searched Porter at school and found a box cutter, which they viewed as a weapon, and they suddenly viewed Porter as a great security risk. In reality, Porter used the box cutter at his part-time job at a grocery store, where he cut open boxes.

"Adam spent four nights in jail," his mother said. "It was unbelievable. Adam never had discipline problems in school. The only complaint I ever received about him was that he sometimes made the other kids laugh, sort of like a class clown. He was one of the most docile kids in school."

Porter was allowed to enroll at an alternative school after his mother waived his right to a hearing on the expulsion proceedings. His mother signed the waiver after being told by a school hearing officer that such school proceedings were regularly decided in the school's favor. Porter attended the alternative school, later reenrolled at East Ascension, and then dropped out in March 2002.

At that time, Adam Porter and his brother sued the Ascension Parish School Board, alleging several constitutional violations, including a First Amendment claim. They asserted that school officials punished them for the content of their artistic expression, which did not constitute a true threat. School officials countered that they could reasonably believe the drawing constituted a true threat or could substantially disrupt school activities.

When the case proceeded to court, federal district court judge Frank J. Polozola had Columbine on his mind and he bluntly wrote as much in his opinion. "School officials," he wrote, "cannot operate in a vacuum or in a fantasy world and must be aware of the events occurring at other schools to properly protect their students and faculty." He concluded that Porter's drawing constituted a true threat.

Porter and his lawyer, Dan Scheuermann, had argued that the drawing could not constitute a true threat because Porter never intended to show it to anyone at school. "This does not and should not matter," Polozola wrote. "What does matter is that the drawing did end up in the hands of a student, a bus driver and school administrators, all of whom were justified in believing it was a threat to the safety of all of the EAHS school family and facilities."

Porter appealed to the U.S. Court of Appeals for the Fifth Circuit—a court that had been transformed through the years by conservative appointees. This was no longer the Fifth Circuit of the jurists who had been dubbed "Unlikely Heroes." It was not the Fifth Circuit that had decided *Burnside v. Byars* and other historic civil rights cases in the 1960s. This was a law and order court—and it showed.

Even this conservative court, however, believed that school officials had overreacted. The Fifth Circuit wrote that "private writings made and kept in one's home enjoy the protections of the First Amendment, as well as the Fourth. . . . For such writings to lose their First Amendment protection, something more than their accidental and unintentional exposure to public scrutiny must take place."

However, the appeals court still ruled in favor of the school officials by granting them qualified immunity. Qualified immunity is a doctrine that protects government officials from liability in civil rights actions when they do not violate clearly established principles of law. The panel wrote that a reasonable school official "facing this question for the first time would find no pre-existing body of law from which he could draw clear guidance and certain conclusions."

Because of the "unsettled nature of First Amendment law as applied to off-campus student speech inadvertently brought on campus by others," the court determined that the school officials did not violate clearly established constitutional rights.

Porter's mother took little solace in the Fifth Circuit's finding that Porter's drawing had First Amendment protection. She believed that the school officials did not deserve any type of immunity. "The very first thing we learn in studying the Constitution is that you cannot be punished for voicing your opinion, or otherwise expressing yourself," she said. "And the sanctity of the home is well established. It is not logical to believe that a rational adult—a school principal, no less—would not know this."

For this reason, the Rutherford Institute continued to fund the case in an unsuccessful attempt to bring it before the U.S. Supreme

Court. "The [Supreme] Court really needs to look at whether quali-fied immunity trumps First Amendment rights in these kinds of cases," Whitehead said before the high court refused to hear the case in spring 2005.

Adam Porter later obtained his G.E.D. and, according to his mother, began working in a four-year apprentice program to become a sheet worker.

DEAR DIARY

Even private diaries are not safe from the long arm of some school officials, as the Ponce family in El Paso, Texas, can readily attest. En-rique and Rocio Ponce sued the school district for suspending their son—known in court papers as "E. P."—for content in his diary. E. P., who was fascinated with World War II movies and books, had cre-ated a work of fiction about a group of Nazi-like kids who injured two gays and seven "colored" people. E. P.'s mother had attended a college creative writing course and then encouraged her son to write creatively—though she did not encourage his choice of topic.

E. P. showed the work to a classmate, who alerted Montwood High School assistant principal Jesus Aguirre. The official searched E. P.'s book bag and found a green spiral notebook with the title "My Nazi Diary Based on a True Story." Aguirre then sent E. P. back to class. However, after further review of the diary, the picture changed for E. P. Aguirre not only suspended E. P. for making a "terroristic threat" but also called the El Paso Police Department to have the student arrested. After reviewing the case, the district attorney's of-fice declined to prosecute.

The Ponces moved their son to a private school and sued the school district for violation of E. P.'s First Amendment rights. Law-yers for the school district sought to dismiss the lawsuit, but U.S. district judge Kathleen Cardone rejected their efforts and ruled in favor of the Ponces.

Cardone analyzed the case under the familiar *Tinker*, *Fraser*, and *Hazelwood* trilogy. She easily found *Fraser* and *Hazelwood* inappli-cable, because the student writing contained no lewd or sexual expression and was not school sponsored. According to Cardone, the case should be evaluated under the *Tinker* standard—whether school officials could reasonably forecast that E. P.'s diary would cause a substantial disruption. She wondered how school officials could view the diary as a disruptive influence when Aguirre had immediately sent the student back to class: "This Court is left pondering how Defendant can establish a reasonable belief that E. P.'s notebook would cause material and substantial disruption to the operation of the school, and that it was of such character so as to threaten the 'safety and security [of] the students,' when Aguirre immediately returned E. P. to the very population that E. P. had purportedly 'terrorized.'"

Cardone contrasted the reaction of Aguirre with that of school officials in the James Lavine case—where emergency expulsion proceedings were brought immediately. "In similar cases, wherein courts have affirmed disciplinary actions in the name of student safety, administrators have taken *immediate* action to segregate potentially dangerous students from the rest of the student body," she wrote.

Absent from the El Paso school officials' actions was a consideration as to whether E. P.'s writings were really fiction or whether he was plotting to create any type of Nazi-like group that might inflict damage on other students. School officials didn't ask E. P.'s friends at school about whether he was trying to form a dangerous group or gang. Judge Cardone concluded her analysis with the statement: "Public schools are designed to bestow upon our children a full and fair education, embracing diverse and often contentious viewpoints."

The school district appealed to the Fifth Circuit—the same Fifth Circuit that had ruled against Adam Porter. Seemingly, the school district's appeal would fail, as Judge Cardone had shown in her thoughtful analysis in *Ponce v. Socorro Independent School District* (2007).

However, the school district received a large dose of serendipity in the form of the 2007 U.S. Supreme Court decision *Morse v. Frederick*, a.k.a. "Bong Hits 4 Jesus." Though the Court had ruled that public school officials could restrict any student speech that they reasonably believe promotes illegal drug use, the Fifth Circuit read the case differently, in part by focusing upon a concurring opinion in *Morse* by Justice Samuel Alito. In his concurrence, Alito wrote about the dangers of drug use in a school environment.

The Fifth Circuit in *Ponce v. Socorro Independent School District* extended Alito's analysis to allow school officials greater leeway to regulate any student speech that might pose a safety risk—even if the speech does not constitute a true threat or pose a substantial disruption under *Tinker*. Such an unwarranted application of *Morse* radically changes student speech and puts at grave risk any student speech that discusses themes of violence or that someone interprets (or misinterprets) as a problem.

"While administrators of course must take seriously all threats of school violence, part of taking a threat seriously is evaluating it," wrote legal commentator Douglas Lee in a commentary for the First Amendment Center. "In this case, no evidence existed that the sophomore [E. P.] intended any violence. The fictional nature of the notebook was clear from the fact that the student had not created a pseudo-Nazi group, had not caused any violent incident and described a shooting that was to occur several years in the future. The lack of a credible threat also was clear in the prosecutor's decision not to press criminal charges."

THE NEW REALITY

Unfortunately, the lessons learned from the plights of Christopher Beamon, J. M., James Lavine, Adam Porter, and E. P. are that students possess few First Amendment free speech rights—particularly with regard to any speech that contains violent themes or imagery. Students have been thrown in jail, subjected to intrusive psychological probing, expelled on an emergency basis, and kicked out of school permanently even if they uttered no true threat or caused no substantial disruption. Mary LeBlanc, Adam's Porter's mother, said, "A lesson I learned is that kids in public schools don't have any First Amendment rights. . . . They may think they do, but they don't.

Kids' rights are slipping away in public schools, just as other rights are slipping away in society. And people often don't seem to care or realize that it's happening."

The quandary facing school officials is how to balance school safety with the duty to ensure the protection of students' constitutional rights. This balancing process is difficult and uncertain. Some argue that great deference should be given to school officials, who are in the best position to evaluate the particular student. Others question the policy of silencing any student speech deemed controversial, arguing that silencing students can breed greater alienation and resentment. The fear is that if students feel they have no outlet, they may resort to more subversive, violent means of expressing themselves. Scholars have identified this view as the "safety valve" justification for free speech best articulated by Supreme Court justice Louis Brandeis, who wrote in 1927 that the "path of safety lies in the opportunity to discuss freely supported grievances and proposed remedies."

Judge Kleinfeld subscribed to this safety valve theory of speech when he wrote in his dissent in the *Lavine* case that "suppression of speech may reduce security as well as liberty." Kleinfeld also warned about the dangers of interpreting constitutional principles such as freedom of speech with excessive reliance on headlines about cataclysmic events such as Columbine. "Constitutional law ought to be based on neutral principles, and should not easily sway in the winds of popular concerns, for that would make our liberty a weak reed that swayed in the winds."

School officials can and should examine violent-themed student writing and take action if the student has a track record of mental instability and violent conduct. They are charged with providing a safe learning environment. But the stories of the student litigants in this chapter show that school officials should not engage in an inflexible, knee-jerk-reaction mindset that treats every writer using violent content as the next Dylan Klebold or Seung-Hui Cho. "We do not, under our constitution, allow the government to punish artists for making art, whether the art is good or bad, whether it makes people feel good or bad, unless the expression falls within a well established category of unprotected speech," Judge Kleinfeld wrote. "This right too does not end at the schoolhouse gate."

Unfortunately, some students have had the gate slammed shut in their faces.

CHAPTER 8

THE DRESS DEBATE

David Chalifoux and Jerry Robertson were devout Catholics who attended New Caney High School in Montgomery County, Texas. They never got into trouble at school—until January 1997, when they started wearing rosary beads to express their religious faith. Two school police officers warned them that the beads were considered gang-related apparel. The officers told the two students that they had to either remove the beads or tuck them under their shirts out of view. The two students were shocked; they had never been mistaken for gang members before and had never associated with gang members.

The school handbook listed some sample gang-related items, including bandannas, oversized trousers, hairnets, and sweatbands. Rosaries were not included on the list. School officials claimed, however, that the list needed to be flexible, as gangs frequently adopt different symbols. One of the officers identified rosaries as gang related after receiving information that some members of the gang United Homies were wearing rosaries.

After hearing the lawsuit brought by the two students, who challenged the ban on rosaries, U.S. district judge David Hittner viewed the case differently from the police officers. Hittner applied a two-part legal test often used to determine whether student conduct—including student apparel—is expressive enough to even merit initial First Amendment review. Under the first part of this legal test, the student must show an intent to convey a particularized message.

This requirement—while it sounds easy—had often tripped up students' free speech claims in the past. For example, Richard Bivens, a New Mexico teen, lost his First Amendment challenge to a ban on sagging pants because a federal judge there determined that there was no particularized message in the wearing of baggy (or sagging) pants. In *Bivens v. Albuquerque Public Schools* (1995), the judge questioned whether sagging pants conveyed any particular message: "Sagging is not necessarily associated with any single racial or cultural group, and sagging is seen by some merely as a fashion trend followed by many adolescents all over the United States." The judge further said that even if sagging somehow constituted a message, the student failed to pass the second part of the test—whether a reasonable observer would understand the particularized message.

In the rosaries case, Judge Hittner believed that Chalifoux and Robertson passed this initial "particularized message" hurdle. The wearing of rosaries indicated support of their religious faith— Catholicism. In his opinion in *Chalifoux v. New Caney Independent School District* (1997), Hittner also wrote that observers would reasonably understand the message that the two students were trying to convey. "Even assuming that some persons are not familiar with the rosary, undoubtedly they are familiar with the crucifix attached to the center of the rosary, which is recognized universally as a symbol of Christianity," the judge wrote. "Accordingly, there is a great likelihood that those persons unable to associate Plaintiffs' rosaries with Catholicism nevertheless, will understand that Plaintiffs are Christians."

The judge then had to determine the proper legal test for deciding what constituted a regulation of the students' religious expression. The students argued for the application of the *Tinker* test—that the school officials could not ban rosaries unless they could point to some specialized evidence that rosary beads were causing a substantial disruption of school activities. The school officials countered that the proper test to apply came from an earlier antiwar protest case—*United States v. O'Brien* (1968)—where the Court had ruled against a First Amendment challenge by a draft protester who burned his draft card on the steps of a South Boston courthouse. The deferential *O'Brien* test provides that a regulation impacting both speech and nonspeech elements is constitutional if: (1) the government had the power to enact the law; (2) the government has a substantial interest in the law or policy; (3) the government's interest in regulating the action is unrelated to the suppression of free expression; and (4) the restriction on speech is incidental and not an excessive burden on First Amendment freedoms.

Hittner ruled that the *Tinker* "substantial disruption" test applied because—like the black armbands in *Tinker*—the wearing of the rosary beads was "akin to pure speech." Once *Tinker* was chosen as the appropriate basis for analysis, applying it was easy, as school officials "failed to show any evidence of hostility from students at New Caney High School or any other threat of interference with school safety."

The lessons of the *Chalifoux* case haven't been learned by some administrators. In May 2010, school officials at Oneida Middle School in Schenectady, New York, suspended thirteen-year-old Raymond Hosier for wearing a rosary with purple-colored beads. Hosier wore the beads for religious reasons and to mourn the loss of his brother and uncle.

With assistance from the American Center for Law and Justice, Hosier filed a federal lawsuit alleging a violation of his First Amendment rights. In his complaint, he contends that the school's dress code policy is too vague and too broad. He also argues that it infringes on his ability to freely exercise his religious beliefs. In September 2010, the school announced that it would change its policy to allow students to wear rosary beads and other items for religious reasons.

SAFETY MEASURES

While the claims of the school police officers about dangerous rosary beads may seem extreme, the concept of regulating student dress to improve school safety has significant traction and, of course, everyday consequences. Fear of gangs and juvenile "super-predators," along with cases of students being victimized for their high-priced tennis shoes or other sought-after items, has led to drastic changes in how schools treat anyone wearing clothing associated with crime, whether the dress was considered a sign of gang membership or a temptation to would-be thieves. In the war against gang influences in school, student dress often becomes a casualty.

One way many school districts across the country have sought to make schools safer is by implementing formal dress codes and even uniform requirements. A typical uniform policy requires students to wear certain clothes, such as white shirts and blue pants. A dress code policy generally states what type of clothes a student may *not* wear. Standard dress codes will usually forbid T-shirts with sexual slogans, profane language, or advertisements for tobacco or alcohol products, short shorts, torn jeans, sagging jeans, spandex, halter tops, and clothes that expose the midriff.

Many public schools adopted such dress codes or uniforms after then president Bill Clinton endorsed uniforms in his 1996 State of the Union address:

> I challenge all our schools to teach character education, to teach good values and good citizenship. And if it means that teenagers will stop killing each other over designer jackets, then our public schools should be able to require their students to wear school uniforms. If it means that the schoolrooms will be more orderly, more disciplined and that our young people will learn to evaluate themselves by what they are on the inside instead of what they're wearing on the outside, then our public schools should be able to require their students to wear school uniforms.

Shortly after this address, Clinton ordered the Department of Education to issue manuals on the importance and effectiveness of school uniforms. The Department of Education distributed its *Manual on School Uniforms* to more than sixteen thousand school districts nationwide. The manual stated that school uniforms represent "one positive and creative way to reduce discipline problems and increase student safety." The handbook also provided that "in response to growing levels of violence in our schools, many parents, teachers, and school officials have come to see school uniforms as one positive and creative way to reduce discipline problems and increase school safety."

Clinton cited the impressive results of a mandatory school uniform policy in Long Beach, California, that was adopted in 1994 district-wide after a successful pilot program with uniforms was implemented at eleven schools the previous year. Other school districts, such as Los Angeles, had seen individual schools adopt dress codes, but Long Beach became the first to make uniforms a district-wide priority. Long Beach Unified School District reported a marked reduction in school disciplinary problems and a significant decline in school crime after instituting its mandatory school uniform policy. For example, in the school's "Grades K–8 School Crime Report Summary," the number of reported sex offenses was shown to have dropped from fifty-seven to fifteen during the first year of uniforms. Similarly, the number of assault and battery crimes dropped from 319 to 214.

And yet despite some positive experiments with implementing uniforms, one study found that uniforms do *not* lead to better discipline in schools. A study by David Brunsma, arguably the leading authority on uniforms in the country, and Kerry Rocquemore concluded that "student uniforms have no direct effect on substance abuse, behavioral problems or attendance." They added that "a negative effect of uniforms on student academic achievement was found."

"GANG-RELATED APPAREL"

The controversy over whether or not controlling student dress actually improves safety continues in the twenty-first century. A major impetus for school uniforms in Long Beach and other locations was to reduce the problems associated with gangs and gang-related violence. In June 2008, Los Angeles issued a press release discussing new school uniform policies in light of a continuing gang problem: "Today, in the City of Los Angeles, there are 39,000 gang members—many of whom are harming kids in and around school campuses simply because of the clothes they are wearing." Los Angeles specifically touted the successes of uniform policies in not only Long Beach but also Washington, D.C., Philadelphia, and San Diego.

Some commentators firmly believe that dress codes and uniforms can directly reduce violence. They argue that schools should ban certain types of clothing, such as trench coats and baggy pants, that enable students to hide weapons easily. A dress code or uniform policy also prevents students from wearing gang-related apparel and colors, which was the main reason that many schools adopted dress codes in the first place. Some state laws empower school officials to ban gang-related apparel specifically. The California Education Code, section 35183, asserts that "gang-related apparel is hazardous to the health and safety of the school environment." It further empowers school districts to adopt uniforms at their discretion: "The adoption of a schoolwide uniform policy is a reasonable way to provide some protection for students. A required uniform may protect students from being associated with any particular gang. Moreover, by requiring schoolwide uniforms teachers and administrators may not need to occupy as much of their time learning the subtleties of gang regalia."

In 1994, Tennessee passed a law empowering school districts to adopt measures to combat gangs in school. This measure was used by some schools to implement dress codes or prohibitions as broad as banning blue or red clothing. Iowa adopted a similar policy the next year empowering individual schools to address the problem. Iowa's law states in part that "gang-related apparel worn at school draws attention away from the school's learning environment and directs it toward thoughts or expressions of violence, bigotry, hate, and abuse." In 1997, the state of Washington also enacted a law giving schools the power to regulate gang-related apparel.

While the need to address gang-related problems is understandable, many disagree fundamentally over the merits of regulating student dress as a principal way to address larger societal problems. Proponents of dress codes and uniforms argue they reduce violence, lessen peer pressure, create a more positive learning environment, promote unity of spirit, and do not violate the constitutional rights of students and their parents. Dress codes and uniforms improve safety by allowing school officials to more easily distinguish students from nonstudents on school grounds, preventing trespassers who might cause harm at the school. Students may be spared ostracism because they cannot afford the latest fashions that are popular among their classmates. Others believe that dress codes decrease student-to-student sexual harassment and help prepare students for being part of the workforce. Some school administrators say that such restrictions help prepare students to "dress for success" in the job market.

Opponents of such measures counter that uniforms and restrictive dress suppress student individuality and personal freedom. They argue that students could become alienated if school officials close off one of their few avenues of self-identification and expression. They also question whether restrictive dress codes actually make schools safer or serve as only a band-aid. Some commentators have questioned whether certain dress code policies will disproportionally impact minority students. For example, legal commentator Paul Murphy wrote that "dress codes may contain an inherent racial bias because they tend to focus on clothing associated with African-American gangs while ignoring other groups such as white supremacist gangs." Many parents argue that these restrictive policies also infringe on their liberty interests in rearing their children as they see fit.

TINKER AND STUDENT DRESS?

As the rosary cases demonstrated, the initial question often raised in student free expression cases is whether the student has even engaged in free expression. We know that if a student is punished for the spoken or written word, the First Amendment is implicated. The student engaged in speech. But does the First Amendment apply to more than just verbal communication or the printed word?

The *Tinker* decision obviously centered on expressive conduct, the wearing of black armbands, that deserved free speech protection. In *Spence v. Washington* (1974), the U.S. Supreme Court established a two-part test for determining whether expressive conduct merits First Amendment protection. First, the expressive conduct had to convey a particularized message. Second, the message had to be one that many people would likely understand. Recall that judges had applied this very test in both the sagging pants and rosary beads cases.

Proponents of dress code and uniform policies argue that a great deal of student clothing does not qualify as expressive conduct because it doesn't contain a particularized message. On the other hand, they may also argue that dress code policies are passed for legitimate reasons connected to a message; for instance, if students wear "White Power" T-shirts, a school official could reasonably forecast that the T-shirts will exacerbate racial tensions at the school and cause a substantial disruption of school activities. We've seen students punished for wearing Confederate flag garb to school; if the school has any sort of racial tension, the students generally lose the free speech argument.

Ironically, both opponents and proponents of student dress codes point to *Tinker* to support their positions. Dress code opponents emphasize the broad message of *Tinker*—that schools cannot censor student expression unless they can show a substantial disruption. They point out that students convey a multitude of messages in how they dress and what they wear on their clothing, including political slogans, personal mantras, religious beliefs, and support for a favorite athletic team. They argue that school officials cannot censor student expression unless they can show that the clothing will disrupt the school environment. They contend that *Tinker* stands for the fundamental principle that students have the right to wear clothing with messages, just as the students in the 1960s could wear black armbands to protest the Vietnam War.

However, those who favor dress codes cite another passage from *Tinker*: "The problem posed by the present case does not relate to regulation of the length of skirts or the type of clothing, to hair style or deportment." Opponents seize on this language to emphasize that even *Tinker* recognized that disputes over types of clothing do not raise the same free speech interests as regulation of the type of expression at issue with armbands. In *Tinker*, they point out, the Supreme Court distinguished controversy over more typical clothing from the wearing of black armbands, which the Court regarded as a form of political protest involving "direct, primary First Amendment rights akin to 'pure speech.'"

Still, if the "expression" on student clothing constitutes pure political speech, the student has at least a good chance of convincing school officials—if not a reviewing judge—that it should be tolerated or it will be protected by the courts.

In 2003, Michigan high school student Bretton Barber successfully obtained a preliminary injunction in a federal district court that prevented school officials from banning his T-shirt showing a photograph of President George W. Bush with the words INTERNATIONAL TERRORIST. U.S. district judge Patrick J. Duggan ruled in October 2003 in favor of the student in *Barber v. Dearborn Public Schools* because, he said, school officials had silenced Barber's expression more out of a dislike of its message than fear that it might disrupt school. In other words, Duggan applied the *Tinker* standard and determined that the school officials failed to meet that test. In fact, the judge compared Barber's shirt opposing President Bush's policies in Iraq to the students from *Tinker* who opposed the Vietnam War. He reasoned that the students in *Tinker* were engaging in antiwar political speech—dissenting from official U.S. policy in Vietnam. Bretton Barber was engaging in the type of expression that the Founding Fathers most desired to protect.

"Clearly the tension between students who support and those who oppose President Bush's decision to invade Iraq is no greater than the tension that existed during the United States' involvement in Vietnam between supporters of the war and war-protestors," Duggan wrote, adding that "students benefit when school officials provide an environment where they can openly express their diverging viewpoints and when they learn to tolerate the opinions of others."

Perhaps an even more surprising example of a pro-student ruling occurred when a federal appeals court ruled in *Guiles v. Marineau* (2006) that thirteen-year-old Zachary Guiles had a First Amendment right to wear a "chicken hawk" T-shirt mocking President George W. Bush. The T-shirt that the student from Williamsburg, Vermont, wore featured images of alcohol and lines of cocaine, implying that the president was a former alcohol and drug abuser. The court found that the shirt was not disruptive of school activities or offensive enough to warrant regulation given that the images on the shirt were part of a "political, anti-drug message." The Second Circuit's decision was interesting, as many would view the shirt more as a direct insult to the sitting president than a condemnation of illegal drugs.

"DRUGS SUCK"

Uncertainty abounds over the precise contours of acceptable student dress from a First Amendment perspective. Some courts have applied the more school-administrator-friendly standard from *Bethel v. Fraser* (1986) where Matthew Fraser's sexually laced speech led the Supreme Court to rule that school officials could restrict student speech that is vulgar, lewd, or plainly offensive. Many student dress cases are evaluated through the prism of *Fraser* instead of *Tinker*. In February 1992, Kimberly Ann Broussard faced such an evaluation as a well-intentioned middle school student from Norfolk, Virginia. She had purchased a T-shirt bearing the message DRUGS SUCK at a New Kids On The Block concert in 1991. Broussard wore the shirt to school several times without incident. However, another time she wore the shirt, a teacher stopped her in the hallway and told her it was inappropriate. Later, the principal told Broussard and her mother that the shirt could not be worn because it had sexual connotations.

Broussard, with assistance from the Virginia ACLU, sued the school officials, contending a violation of her free expression and due process rights. The federal district court held a hearing on the matter and heard testimony from Broussard, whom the court described as a "mature young lady of thirteen." She testified that she purchased the shirt because she believed drugs were a problem and that more young people her age needed to hear an antidrug message at school. School officials, however, were hung up on the verb *sucks*.

In what must have been a high point in American jurisprudence, each side presented experts that testified as to the etymology and meaning of the word *sucks*. Plaintiff's expert, Duke University professor Dr. Ronald Butters, testified that the word in this context meant that drugs are bad. He distinguished between the transitive usage of the word, which had sexual connotations, and the intransitive usage of the word, which simply meant disapproval. The school presented as their experts Dr. Carol Johnson, a professor from Virginia Wesleyan University, who testified that the word had a sexual connotation in most usages, and Dr. Ulysses Spiva, who testified that the word *suck* would create disturbances at school.

The court determined that "a reasonable middle school administrator could find that the word 'suck,' even as used on the shirt, may be interpreted to have a sexual connotation." The court then relied on the *Fraser* standard to find that school officials could ban the T-shirt because the word *sucks* was a vulgar and lewd term. "The Supreme Court has given great deference to school boards, as in *Fraser*," the judge wrote. "Recent cases have evidenced a concern for values and decency in addition to school order." Steve Pershing, lawyer for Broussard, said that she and her family had decided not to appeal.

CONFUSION

As the *Chalifoux* and *Broussard* cases demonstrate, the legal tests for evaluating restrictions on student dress are less than clear. Some courts will apply the *Tinker* "substantial disruption" standard, while others apply the "lewd, indecent or offensive speech" standard from *Fraser*.

Still other courts will apply standards that are not unique to the student speech arena. Consider the case of Alan Newsom in Albemarle County, Virginia, who proudly wore a "Shooting Sports Camp" T-shirt that had a picture of two guns on it. Newsom had attended a camp with his father, where he shot skeet and took part in related activities. However, a school administrator—in a post-Columbine environment—reacted negatively to the shirt and cited Newsom with a dress code violation. The school's dress code prohibited any type of clothing that "relates to weapons." In a lawsuit funded by the National Rifle Association, Newsom sued, contending a violation of his First Amendment rights. A federal district court judge ruled against Newsom in his lawsuit against school officials and its dress code policy.

Newsom appealed to the Fourth U.S. Circuit, pressing the argument that the dress code policy violated a fundamental doctrine of constitutional law known as overbreadth. A law is unconstitutionally overbroad if it sweeps too broadly and prohibits protected speech in addition to unprotected speech. While a dress code prohibiting references to weaponry might prohibit some speech that perhaps should be censored, the school's policy also went too far. The Fourth Circuit pointed out that the dress code provision technically prohibited students from wearing any T-shirt with the state seal of Virginia because it contains a picture of a woman with a spear and a sword standing over a tyrant. It also would prohibit the student from wearing a jersey with the University of Virginia's mascot, because the mascot—the Cavalier—has two sabers. The mascot of the county high school—located right across the street from Newsom's middle school—is a Patriot carrying a musket. Thus, the appeals court in *Newsom v. Albemarle County School Board* (2003) deemed the dress code provision too broad and struck it down.

BACK TO UNIFORMS

Some school districts, of course, follow the Long Beach School District model and adopt uniform policies that prohibit individual messages and strictly regulate student garb. These policies have received favor at least from some courts. For example, the U.S. Court of Appeals for the Fifth Circuit upheld a Texas school district's uniform policy in *Littlefield v. Forney Independent School District* and a Louisiana school district's similar policy in *Canady v. Bossier Parish School Board*.

School officials in these cases claimed they adopted uniforms to create a more learning-friendly environment free from disruptions and other problems. They also argued the policies would improve students' academic performance, raise self-esteem, and decrease violence, and perhaps lessen socioeconomic tensions between students who had money to purchase expensive clothes and those who did not.

The appeals court determined that these were valid reasons for establishing the policies and that the school districts were not trying to suppress free expression—the key legal point from the *O'Brien* test.

In 2008, another federal appeals court—this time the Ninth Circuit—upheld a broad uniform policy in Clark County, Nevada, in *Jacobs v. Clark County School District*. Kimberly Jacobs and other students challenged the uniform policy in part because it prohibited any message-bearing clothing—even political messages. The students argued that this violated the spirit of *Tinker*, which had protected the political message associated with the antiwar armbands.

But the school district argued—and the court agreed—that *Tinker* was not a proper precedent, because it only applied to school policies that discriminated against student speech based on its particular viewpoint. Recall that one reason the Court invalidated the black armband ban was that the school selectively singled out the black armbands and allowed the Iron Cross and other symbols.

In *Jacobs*, the court held that the uniform policy was not designed to suppress any particular message or viewpoint. But its net effect was to wipe out an incredibly broad range of student speech.

LET THE STUDENTS PROTEST

Even though several courts have upheld school uniform policies, they also recognize that students retain the right to demonstrate against dress code policies by wearing protest logos or armbands.

Even the Department of Education's *Manual on School Uniforms* says that students retain the right to protest.

The Watson Chapel School District in Arkansas found this out the hard way after officials there punished students for wearing black armbands to protest the adoption of a dress code in 2006. A group of students and parents opposed to the policy handed out black armbands to students to wear to school. School officials suspended the students for having the audacity to disagree with official school policy. The students sued in federal court, arguing that *Tinker* protected their right to protest school policy just as it did John Tinker in protesting the Vietnam War.

The case eventually reached the U.S. Court of Appeals for the Eighth Circuit, which issued a stinging rebuke to the school officials in *Lowry v. Watson Chapel School District* (2008). The school officials contended that *Tinker* was inapplicable, because the protest in that case dealt with an important world political issue of interest to the larger community, while the students in Watson Chapel were only protesting something of interest to some people in the local community.

"Whether student speech protests national foreign policy or local school board policy is not constitutionally significant," the Eighth Circuit wrote. We find defendants' attempts to meaningfully distinguish *Tinker* unconvincing. We hold that *Tinker* is so similar in all constitutionally relevant facts that its holding is dispositive. In both cases, a school district punished students based on their non-disruptive protest of a government policy."

Dress remains a key outlet for students' self-identity and self-expression. Much of this expression does not cause disruptions or disturbances. School officials should not be able to censor student expression under a dress code policy unless they can demonstrate that it will cause a substantial disruption of school activities. However, a strong push to adopt uniforms and more restrictive dress codes leads to the suppression of much student speech.

The courts are hopelessly divided on the proper legal standard for evaluating dress code disputes. They cannot even agree on the fundamental meaning and application of *Tinker*, still the seminal U.S. Supreme Court case on student speech.

While the legal landscape remains muddled, the picture remains clear: dress code disputes will continue to arise in different school districts and communities. Parents often feel just as passionately as their children—if not more so—about what the kids can, and can't, wear to school.

CHAPTER 9
THE NEW FRONTIER

In the 1990s, the world of communication forever changed with the advent of a powerful new medium and tool that enabled people to communicate instantaneously with their friends, colleagues, and even total strangers across the globe. People could post their opinions, thoughts, ideas, and rants on the Internet and the user-friendly World Wide Web. They could use electronic mail in place of expensive long-distance phone calls. People entered the blogosphere, posting their own analysis of everything from news events to products, films, and sports events. Everyone had the potential to become a pamphleteer. The world saw, in the words of federal judge Stewart Dalzell, "a far more speech-enhancing medium than print, the village green, or the mails."

But the Internet amplified all forms of speech—the good, the bad, and the ugly. Pornography, obscenity, hate speech, true threats, vile gossip, defamation, and other forms of unprotected or unfavored speech had free reign in the new medium. U.S. legislators responded as regulators have done throughout history when confronted with a revolutionary new medium—they sought to censor and control it. Shortly after Gutenberg invented the printing press in the fifteenth century, religious officials created censorship bureaus and the Venice Inquisition issued the first list of banned books. When movies entered public awareness in the early twentieth century—including film of the brash black heavyweight champion Jack Johnson thrashing the former white champion James J. Jeffries, which led to calls to ban fight films—the Supreme Court found no First Amendment protection for film, agreeing the new medium would be particularly effective in corrupting youth. Prominent First Amendment attorney Robert Corn Revere has referred to this regrettable pattern as the "culture of regulation."

The "culture of regulation" continued when the Internet and World Wide Web became prevalent, as the U.S. Congress in 1996 hastily amended a large telecommunications deregulation bill to include something that became known as the Communications Decency Act (CDA). Provisions in the bill criminalized the online transmission of "patently offensive" or "indecent" speech. Obviously, supporters of the CDA sought to wield the law as a weapon against the scourge of online pornography. However, the wording of the law to include "indecent" speech affected far more than commercial pornography. Technically it might apply to an e-mail with profane language, pictures of breast cancer patients, or an article about the dangers of prison rape.

The American Civil Liberties Union and the American Library Association challenged the law in federal court in separate lawsuits. Collectively, the lawsuits eventually reached the U.S. Supreme Court. In June 1997, the Supreme Court ruled in *Reno v. ACLU* that the questioned provisions of the CDA impermissibly restricted the free speech rights of adults in order to protect minors.

The federal government had argued that the Internet was entitled to less First Amendment protection than the print media (such as newspapers) and should be treated similarly to broadcast radio and television, which was entitled to less protection. The Court rejected that argument and determined that the Internet was instead entitled to the highest degree of First Amendment protection. In the words of the late attorney Bruce Ennis, who argued the case before the Court on behalf of the ACLU, the decision gave the Internet its "legal birth certificate."

In 1998 Congress would pass a narrower criminal law called the

Child Online Protection Act (COPA) that criminalized the online transmission of material that was "harmful to minors." The Court invalidated that law as well, in part because it found that federal law requiring Internet filters, known as the Children's Internet Protection Act (CIPA), was a less speech-restrictive alternative. The Court in *United States v. American Library Association* (2003) had upheld the constitutionality of this federal law requiring public schools and libraries that received federal funding for Internet hookups to install blocking software to protect minors. Even though studies had been done showing that the filtering technologies often blocked too much material, the Court upheld the measure in a lawsuit brought on behalf of libraries, not schools.

The Court, led by Chief Justice William Rehnquist, reasoned that using filtering software that blocked pornography was no different than a public library deciding not to acquire pornographic materials for its collection. "Public library staffs necessarily consider content in making collection decisions and enjoy broad discretion in making them," Rehnquist explained.

Because the Children's Internet Protection Act requires public schools to install blocking software, it has raised interesting issues for students and teachers. Sometimes the filters block important information students need to complete school assignments. John Bowen, a former high school educator in Ohio, said the filters hindered education rather than protecting children from harm. He explained that he had his school "permanently remove them [the filters] for the journalism rooms and students." Too often, students were not able to access important information about health issues or prison conditions because of these filters. Bowen, who is currently an adjunct professor and assistant director of Kent State University's Center for Scholastic Journalism, recalled that he had to call to have the filters removed because "one of my students was doing a story on something that involved him having to go to the Student Press Law Center [SPLC] for background. That day it was blocked because the filter did not like one of the SPLC's news flashes on a publication being censored at another school somewhere else in the country. So, the SPLC was blocked." As this anecdote shows, the filters often block too much information and can harm the educational mission.

While the battle over filtering the Internet remains an important issue, perhaps the most important issue for students today concerns their ability to express themselves online. Many students have been punished for their online speech even if they posted the material on a blog or social networking site off campus. As social networking sites such as MySpace, Xanga, and Facebook grew in popularity, the conflict with would-be censors intensified. Most content created by students online presents no First Amendment or disciplinary problems. Students routinely write about their favorite musicians, athletes, video games, or television shows, or other matters important to their daily lives. But occasionally students post material about classmates, teachers, or administrators that can pose problems. It could be students posting false and damaging statements about a school official, an alienated student creating a list of students he would like to see harmed, or a student spewing vulgar and lewd content. Many students' hallway gossip and telephone rants are now posted online for the world to see. At times criminal authorities have used material placed online to attempt to thwart Columbine-style planned violence. Five students in Kansas were arrested in April 2006, for example, for an alleged plot to engage in a murderous spree on the seven-year anniversary of the infamous Columbine shootings.

SPEECH AT THE SHOPPING MALL

While student online speech battles are the current rage, the underlying controversy over off-campus speech goes back decades if not longer. For years, school officials have struggled with the question of how far their authority reaches. They have grappled with whether they can punish a student for obnoxious, offensive expression off campus, like at a nearly shopping mall.

On a Sunday in May 1976, Marion Center High School student Jeffrey Fenton sat in a car with several friends outside North Plaza, a popular shopping mall in Indiana, Pennsylvania. Donald Stear, a teacher at Marion, passed by the car. One student in the car stated, "There's Stear." Fenton replied loudly enough for Stear to hear: "He's a prick."

That intemperate comment uttered off campus merited Fenton a three-day in-school suspension from the vice principal. An in-school suspension consisted of the student sitting alone in a small classroom—called "jail" by the students—for the entire day with no instruction, a punishment reminiscent of John Hughes's famous 1985 movie *The Breakfast Club*, except Fenton had no other students around him. School officials further punished Fenton by not allowing him to attend the senior class trip. Later, school officials extended the suspension to seven more days and Fenton had to sit in the cafeteria in isolation during lunch period. He served out his suspension and graduated without incident. He then sued in federal court, contending that school officials violated his First Amendment rights by punishing him for his off-campus expression.

The federal court disagreed in *Fenton v. Stear* (1976), reasoning that Fenton's name-calling did merit punishment by school officials. "It is our opinion that when a high school student refers to a high school teacher in a public place on a Sunday by a lewd and obscene name in such a loud voice that the teacher and others hear the insult it may be deemed a matter for discipline in the discretion of the school authorities," the judge wrote. "To countenance such student conduct even in a public place without imposing sanctions could lead to devastating consequences in the school." The judge then explained that if school officials erred and exceeded their jurisdiction, any such error was "de minimis," or minimal. Missing a senior trip, in the words of the court, does not qualify as the loss of a constitutionally protected right.

"Frankly I think that what a student does on his or her own time off campus with respect to expression or expressive conduct is his or her own business and not subject to discipline by school authorities," said attorney Jay Y. Rubin, who represented Fenton in the case. "If a student engages in expressive conduct that might constitute criminal conduct, then it is a matter for law enforcement. If not, then it is a matter for parents or guardians. . . . Punishing students for off-campus conduct or expression doesn't help to maintain discipline."

"DIGITAL POSTURING"

In April 1986 public school teacher Clyde Clark drove his son to a local restaurant in South Paris, Maine, so that he could apply for a job there. As he waited for his son to return, another car parked near his. A passenger in that car, student Jason Klein, gave Clark the middle-digit salute, or "the finger." Klein then proceeded to exit the car and enter the restaurant.

Clark reported the incident to his principal, who suspended Jason Klein for ten days under a school rule prohibiting "vulgar or extremely inappropriate language or conduct directed to a staff member." Klein sought the services of a lawyer and contested the charges. He argued that the school had no authority to discipline him for purely off-campus expressive conduct.

The case came before federal district court judge Gene Carter, who was nominated to the federal bench in 1983 by President Ronald Reagan. A former state court judge with much army reserve experience, Judge Carter was not a likely candidate on the surface to issue a ruling in favor of a bird-flipping miscreant. The school officials marshaled much support from the teaching ranks. Clark and the chairperson of the English and foreign-language departments at Oxford Hills testified in court that the Klein incident had negatively affected their ability to discipline Klein and other students in school. Sixty other teachers and school officials signed a statement supporting such sentiments. Lawyers for the school principal, Kenneth Smith, contended that the Klein matter had adversely affected the administration of school discipline. They focused their attention on meeting the "substantial disruption" standard of *Tinker*.

In June 1986, Carter began his opinion in *Klein v. Smith* by quoting a passage from Samuel Johnson's *London* (1738):

> Of all the griefs that harass the distress'd,
> Sure the most bitter is a scornful jest;

Fate never wounds more deep the gen'rous heart,
Than when a blockhead's insult points the dart.

In a memorable passage, Carter also rejected the notion that school officials at Oxford Hills High would not be able to enforce discipline because of the unfortunate incident between Jason Klein and Clyde Clark. "The Court cannot do these sixty-two mature and responsible professionals the disservice of believing that collectively their professional integrity, personal mental resolve, and individual character are going to dissolve, willy-nilly, in the face of the digital posturing of this splenetic, bad-mannered little boy." Carter focused on the location of Klein's intemperate expressive conduct: "The conduct in question occurred in a restaurant parking lot, far removed from any school premises or facilities at a time when teacher Clark was not associated in any way with his duties as a teacher." Carter added that Klein was "not engaged in any school activity or associated in any way with school premises or his role as a student."

Carter concluded that the connection of Klein's rude gesture and the orderly operation of the school was "far too attenuated" to support discipline against the student. In another classic phrase, Carter wrote: "The First Amendment protection of freedom of expression may not be made a casualty of the effort to force-feed good manners to the ruffians among us."

INTO THE DIGITAL WORLD

The Jeffrey Fenton and Jason Klein cases reflect different approaches to off-campus student expression. The *Fenton* court believed strongly that failing to punish a student for calling a teacher a name off campus would have deleterious results on discipline in school. Meanwhile, the *Klein* court rejected that notion and considered the off-campus middle-finger salute to be "too attenuated" to school discipline to be significant. It was a matter of parental, not school, discipline.

It is ironic that Judge Carter chose the word *digital* because both the *Klein* and *Fenton* cases provide key judicial precedent for one of the most contentious areas in all of First Amendment jurisprudence—the punishment of students for off-campus online speech. If a student hops on Facebook, MySpace, or some other social networking site and badmouths a teacher, the question becomes whether school officials can punish the student for such off-campus conduct. As with the contradictory opinions in the *Fenton* and *Klein* cases, the courts are in disarray with respect to how to treat off-campus online speech.

FREE SPEECH LESSON FOR A PRINCIPAL

In early 1998, Brandon Beussink, an eleventh-grader at Woodland High School in Marble Hills, Missouri, created a home page with his sister Brittney that was highly critical of the school's administration: "Please welcome to our Fucked Up High School" and "Home of the fucked up Faculty members from Hell." It also had less than flattering comments about the school principal, Yancy Poorman, and computer teacher, Delma Ferrell. Beussink did not use school computers to create the webpage and did not access the material at school.

However, Brandon allowed his friend Amanda Brown to use his home computer. Brown saw the home page in question. Later, she had an argument with Brandon. In retaliation, Brown accessed the home page at school and showed it to Ferrell. The computer teacher was outraged and showed the principal, who also was offended by the vulgarity on the site. The principal then suspended Brandon for five days, later doubling the suspension to ten days. The evidence showed little, if any, disruption in the school as a result of the webpage.

When Beussink met with Poorman, the principal told him to "clean up" his home page or "clear it out." Beussink then removed the home page from the Internet and served his ten-day suspension. Beussink's suspension caused him to violate the school's excessive absenteeism policy, which in turn caused him to receive failing grades in all of his classes during the second semester of his junior year.

Beussink then filed a federal lawsuit, contending that the principal had violated his First Amendment rights by suspending him for off-campus expression that did not cause a substantial disruption of school activities. He sought a preliminary injunction from the court stating that school officials had violated his free speech rights and ordering the school to remove the forced absences from his record. Beussink sensed a disconnect between the Bill of Rights and the Constitution—subjects school officials were teaching in the curriculum—and what actually happened to him in practice. "We study history and we study the Constitution, but the school doesn't seem to think that it applies to them," he said.

During a court hearing, Beussink's lawyer, Stephen M. Ryal, elicited some very important testimony from the principal. Ryal established that the principal immediately decided to punish Beussink without considering whether the webpage had caused any type of real disruption in the school.

RYAL: Now, Mrs. Ferrell, when she came to you, was upset and angry, is that accurate?

POORMAN: I couldn't discern anger, but upset, yes.

RYAL: Did you discern that she was offended?

POORMAN: Yes, sir, I believed her to be.

RYAL: Would you agree with my characterization that she was very upset and offended?

POORMAN: Yes, sir.

RYAL: She was speaking to you rapidly?

POORMAN: Yes, sir.

RYAL: Quite obviously agitated over this home page, is that right?

POORMAN: Yes, sir.

RYAL: And you were, as well, when you saw it?

POORMAN: When I viewed it and it was explained that it had been seen by other students, yes, sir, I was upset.

RYAL: When you saw this home page, Exhibit 1, at that moment you decided that you were going to discipline Brandon, is that accurate?

POORMAN: That there would be some discipline taken, yes sir.

RYAL: You spoke to no students prior to making that
                   decision, is that correct?

POORMAN: To the best of my recollection, no, sir, I did
                   not.

This testimony showed that the principal suspended Beussink because he was outraged and offended by the content of the webpage, not because it had caused a substantial disruption of school activities under *Tinker*. The attorney for the school officials contended that the discipline passed the "reasonable forecast of disruption" test in *Tinker* because other students had discussed the webpage during the school day and it became the subject of conversation.

However, Judge Rodney Sippel saw it differently, noting that the school officials failed to show that the discussions caused commotion in the school hallways or classrooms. "Principal Poorman's testimony does not indicate that he disciplined Beussink based on a fear of disruption or interference with school discipline (reasonable or otherwise)," Judge Sippel wrote in *Beussink v. Woodland IV School District* (1998). "Principal Poorman's own testimony indicates he disciplined Beussink because he was upset by the content of the home page."

Sippel then wrote language that has been cited and quoted in various cases through the years: "Disliking or being upset by the content of a student's speech is not an acceptable justification for limiting student speech under Tinker." Judge Sippel explained that a major purpose of the First Amendment was to protect unpopular speech. He also admonished school officials to practice what they preach with respect to teaching students about the Bill of Rights. Sippel wrote:

> Indeed, it is often provocative and challenging speech, like Beussink's, which is most in need of the protections of the First Amendment. Popular speech is not likely to provoke censure. It is unpopular speech that invites censure. It is unpopular speech which needs the protection of the First Amendment. The First Amendment was designed for this very purpose.

Speech within the school that substantially interferes with school discipline may be limited. Individual student speech which is unpopular but does not substantially interfere with school discipline is entitled to protection.

The public interest is not only served by allowing Beussink's message to be free from censure, but also by giving the students at Woodland High School this opportunity to see the protections of the United States Constitution and the Bill of Rights at work.

MOCK OBITUARIES

In a later case from the state of Washington, a court seemingly questioned whether the "substantial disruption" test even applied at all. Rather, the judge reasoned that the speech may be beyond the control of school officials. The case involved Nick Emmett, a senior at Kentlake High School in Kent, Washington, who had a 3.95 grade-point average and no disciplinary history. The co-captain of the basketball team, Emmett was in many ways an ideal student. However, he ran afoul of school officials after other students informed them about Emmett's "Unofficial Kentlake High Home Page" in February 2000. The site contained several "mock obituaries" written in a tongue-in-cheek manner. Emmett had been inspired to create such online obituaries from a creative writing project the year before in which the students had to write their own obituaries. He included a section that allowed visitors to his website to vote on who would "die" next in a mock obituary.

The site attracted much attention in the community, including an evening television news story that characterized the site as an online "hit list"—which it was not. Later that evening, Emmett removed the site from the Internet. The next day the principal summoned Emmett to his office and told the student that he was instituting emergency expulsion proceedings against him for intimidation, harassment, and disruption of the educational process. The principal even threw in a charge of copyright violation. The principal subsequently reduced the penalty to a five-day suspension and a prohibition against participating in school functions, including basketball games.

Emmett sued in federal court, contending a violation of his First Amendment rights. U.S. district judge John Coughenour agreed with the student in *Emmett v. Kent School District* (2000). The judge considered whether the lawsuit should be evaluated through the prism of the Supreme Court cases *Tinker*, *Fraser*, or *Hazelwood*. The judge easily dispensed with *Fraser*, noting that Emmett did not speak at a school assembly. He also quickly dispatched application of *Hazelwood*, noting that the website was not produced as part of any school assignment. He also rejected application of *Tinker*, because Emmett's speech did not take place on school grounds.

"Although the intended audience was undoubtedly connected to Kentlake High School, the speech was entirely outside of the school's supervision or control," Coughenour wrote. School officials had argued that in light of recent school shootings in Springfield, Oregon, and Littleton, Colorado, school administrators must be given greater leeway to protect students. Coughenour recognized that school officials are in an "acutely difficult position" but reasoned that school officials have "presented no evidence that the mock obituaries and voting on this web site were intended to threaten anyone, did actually threaten anyone, or manifested any violent tendencies whatsoever."

The judge concluded that school officials must allow Nick Emmett to return to school with full privileges and erase any negative marks from his disciplinary history.

PAYING FOR A "HITMAN"

Not all courts have adopted the reasoning of the judges who ruled in favor of Brandon Beussink and Nick Emmett when confronted with off-campus online student speech. The Pennsylvania Supreme Court had different ideas when it ruled on the online speech of Justin Swidler, who created a webpage on his personal computer when he was an eighth-grader at Nitschmann Middle School in the Bethlehem Area School District. Swidler titled his page "Teacher Sux." It consisted of several derogatory and offensive comments about his math teacher, Kathleen Fulmer, and his principal, A. Thomas Kartsotis.

A section of the page, titled "Welcome to Kartsotis Sux," used profanity in describing the principal and claimed that he engaged in sexual relations with a principal from another school. Another section, "Why Fulmer Should Be Fired," criticized Fulmer and compared her to Adolf Hitler. Another section, "Why Should She Die?," contained the following statement: "Take a look at the diagram and the reasons I gave, then give me $20 to help pay for the future." Another section was titled "Fuck You Mrs. Fulmer" and "You Are a Stupid Bitch."

Kartsotis learned about the website and considered the statements as threatening. He contacted the local police and the Federal Bureau of Investigation (FBI). The law enforcement agencies declined to pursue charges against Swidler. However, Kartsotis believed the website had a demoralizing impact on the school community. Math teacher Kathleen Fulmer suffered emotional distress and could not teach for a semester, citing depression and other ailments. At the end of the school year, Kartsotis decided to impose a three-day suspension on the student. He cited three infractions: threat to a teacher, harassment of a teacher and principal, and disrespect to school officials. The school district heard evidence and increased the suspension to ten days. The school district then began expulsion proceedings against Swidler.

Justin's parents, Dr. Howard Swidler and Irene Swidler, believed that school officials overreacted. They characterized their son's online expression as a bad attempt at satire. Dr. Swidler called his son's actions abhorrent but believed that the school district had no authority to expel his son for off-campus activity. The Swidlers sued in a Pennsylvania state court, alleging a violation of Justin's First Amendment rights.

A trial court granted summary judgment to school officials and a three-judge panel of the Commonwealth Court affirmed that finding by a 2–1 vote. The majority contended that the website constituted a material and substantial disruption within the meaning of *Tinker*. However, Judge Rochelle Friedman dissented, writing that the site did not cause any disruption. The Swidlers then appealed to the Pennsylvania Supreme Court.

The Pennsylvania Supreme Court sided with school officials in *J. S. v. Bethlehem Area School District* (2002). Initially, the state high court examined whether Swidler's site constituted a true threat, because true threats receive no First Amendment protection. School district attorneys contended that the site contained threatening language toward Fulmer, emphasizing the payment of $20 for a "hit man." However, the state high court determined that the site was not a true threat. "We believe that the web site, taken as a whole, was a sophomoric, crude, highly offensive and perhaps misguided attempt at humor or parody," the court wrote. "However, it did not reflect a serious expression of intent to inflict harm." The majority pointed out that school officials allowed Swidler to continue attending school for several months after the website controversy. If Swidler had really conveyed a true threat, school officials would not have allowed him to remain in school but would have instituted emergency expulsion proceedings.

Then, the Pennsylvania high court examined whether school officials were justified in punishing Swidler under the *Tinker* substantial disruption standard even though the speech took place off campus. The majority focused on the fact that the website had a sufficient connection to the school campus. "Importantly, the web site was aimed not at a random audience, but at the specific audience of students and others connected with this particular School District," the court wrote. "We hold that where speech that is aimed at a specific school and/or its personnel is brought onto the school campus or accessed at school by its originator, the speech will be considered on-campus speech."

The court then determined that the website caused an actual disruption of the school environment, including the emotional injuries suffered by Fulmer, anxiety expressed by other students, and the harmful impact on morale at school. "The atmosphere of the entire school community was described as that as if a student had died," the court added.

But the court did not rely solely on the *Tinker* substantial disruption test. It also relied on the Matthew Fraser case in which the Supreme Court held that school officials could punish students for lewd and vulgar speech. Swidler's website contained profane, vulgar, and lewd speech within the meaning of the famous *Fraser* decision. Even though Matthew Fraser had spoken at a school assembly, and Swidler spoke online, the Pennsylvania high court focused on the "concern for the school's educational mission" of inculcating good moral values into the students.

The courts in the *Emmett, Beussink,* and *Swidler* cases all used different approaches. The *Beussink* court applied the *Tinker* substantial disruption standard but emphasized that there really must be disruption or a reasonable forecast of disruption, not simply officials being offended. The *Emmett* court simply found that the off-campus online speech was beyond the control and reach of school authorities even though the intended audience was made up of members of the high school community. The *Swidler* court applied both the *Tinker* and *Fraser* decisions, implying that school officials could punish students for any vulgar and lewd online speech and also relying on an elastic understanding of the "intended audience" rationale to find school jurisdiction.

JAMFEST AND A "DOUCHEBAG"

Students continue to find themselves in trouble at school for their online expression as social networking, blogs, and other web-based communities continue to expand. Connecticut teen Avery Doninger found herself embroiled in a high-profile lawsuit after school officials punished her for criticizing a school official online.

The case began in April 2007 when Doninger—then a junior at Lewis S. Mills High School in Burlington, Connecticut—used offensive language on a blog to criticize school officials' handling of JamFest, a battle-of-the-bands event originally scheduled for April 28 but delayed until June 2007 because students were not able to obtain administrative approval to use the school auditorium.

In a blog, Doninger, the junior class secretary, wrote that a school official "got pissed off and decided to just cancel the whole thing all together." She also called Principal Karissa Niehoff a "douchebag." School officials punished Doninger by forbidding her to run for senior class secretary. Doninger sued in July 2007 in state court but the action was removed to federal court. Doninger sought damages and a new election for secretary. She claimed school officials violated her First Amendment rights by punishing her for the online blog and also for refusing to allow her to distribute "Team Avery" T-shirts.

On appeal, a three-judge panel of the U.S. Court of Appeals for the Second circuit affirmed the lower court in *Doninger v. Niehoff* (2008), determining that Doninger should lose her First Amendment claim because school officials did not violate the standard articulated by the U.S. Supreme Court in *Tinker*. The appeals court determined that "Avery's post created a foreseeable risk of substantial disruption to the work and discipline of the school" and characterized her e-mails as "false and misleading." The Second Circuit failed to address the "Team Avery" T-shirt question. The appeals court sent the case down to the federal district court.

On remand, the federal district court addressed new claims by Doninger's attorney that showed that school officials punished the student merely because they were offended by her speech—not because it was disruptive. The judge acknowledged "that there is evidence in the record—particularly when viewed in the light most favorable to [Doninger]—that suggests that Ms. Niehoff may have punished Ms. Doninger because the blog entry was offensive and uncivil and not because of any potential disruption at school." The judge suggested that the dispute over the true motivation for punishing Doninger created a question of fact that ordinarily would prevent the granting of summary judgment.

However, the judge still ruled for school officials because of the doctrine of qualified immunity. The judge determined that because the law concerning punishment of students for off-campus online speech is so hazy and ill defined, it would be unfair to impose monetary damages on school officials. The judge found that the case against school officials over the censorship of the T-shirts could continue.

Whatever the ultimate outcome of her lawsuit, Avery Doninger's dispute with school officials shows the unsettled nature of student speech online. It is not the only unsettled area of student Internet speech. Two more developments have clouded the picture dramatically in recent years: (1) a greater concern over cyberbullying and (2) the increased practice by some school officials of suing students for defamatory statements online.

CYBERBULLYING

In October 2006, thirteen-year-old Megan Meier killed herself after having been the victim of an Internet hoax. Meier thought that several mean statements about her came from "Josh"—a boy that Meier had come to like. After Meier's suicide, it was discovered that "Josh," in fact, was not a real person; he was the creation of a neighbor named Lori Drew, Drew's daughter, and another person. Apparently, they wanted to see what Meier had to say about Drew's daughter. "Josh" initially made nice comments to Meier, but then the boy dumped her, saying "the world would be a better place without you." Meier, who had some history of depression, hanged herself.

Local prosecutors in Missouri declined to prosecute Drew because there really was not a law that covered her awful conduct. However, prosecutors in California got creative and charged her with violating a federal law known as the Computer Fraud and Abuse Act, traditionally used to prosecute hackers and trademark violators. They charged her in California because that was the home base of MySpace, whose terms of use Drew violated in creating the false identity.

In November 2008, a jury convicted Drew of misdemeanor counts of accessing computers without authorization to then inflict emotional distress upon another. In 2009, a federal judge threw out the convictions in *United States v. Drew*. The judge ruled that application of this federal law to *Drew* posed vagueness problems as "normally, breaches of contract are not the subject of criminal prosecution." Drew may have breached a contract with MySpace when creating a false profile, but she did not think that she would be subject to any type of criminal sanction. The court further pointed out that a broad reading of the federal law would make any possible violation of MySpace's terms of agreement a criminal offense: "If every such breach does qualify, then there is absolutely no limitation or criteria as to which of the breaches should merit criminal prosecution."

The Megan Meier tragedy inspired state and federal lawmakers to address the problems of so-called "cyberbullying." In 2003, legal commentator Renee L. Servance identified the problems caused by online harassment in a piece she wrote for the *Wisconsin Law Review*. "Because the Internet offers a far more powerful vehicle for harassment than traditional methods of speech, the invasion of the rights of the targeted individual is more potent."

After the death of Megan Meier, many legislators agreed with this sentiment. Several states have passed anti-cyberbullying laws designed to target those who harass others online. In June 2008, Missouri governor Matt Blunt signed into law an anti-cyberbullying law in his state. The bill amended and increased penalties under the state's existing harassment law. "We must take every step possible to protect our youth and to punish those who want to bring them harm," Blunt said in a written statement. "Social networking sites and technology have opened a new door for criminals and bullies to prey on their victims, especially children."

Congresswoman Linda Sanchez introduced the Megan Meier Cyberbullying Prevention Act of 2009. A key provision of the bill states: "Whoever transmits in interstate or foreign commerce any communication, with the intent to coerce, intimidate, harass, or cause substantial emotional distress to a person, using electronic means to support severe, repeated, and hostile behavior, shall be fined under this title or imprisoned not more than two years, or both."

Testifying before a House subcommittee on crime, Sanchez emphasized the ubiquity of cyberbullying: "Kids can be bullied any hour of the day or night and even in their own homes." Sanchez recognized the difficulties in attempting to craft an anti-cyberbullying law that would be consistent with First Amendment protections: "Instead, I want the law to be able to distinguish between an annoying chain email, a righteously angry political blog post, or a miffed text to an ex-boyfriend—all of which are and should remain legal; and serious, repeated, and hostile communications made with the intent to harm."

Others wonder if it is a wise idea to federalize the criminalization of cyberbullying, thinking that it is better for schools to deal with this problem at the local level. The key question is exactly what constitutes cyberbullying and how much of it actually occurs. "There is a tendency to exaggerate the data with many surveys dealing with Internet issues," said Nancy Willard, founder of the Center for Safe and Effective Internet Use. "Has anyone said something mean to you at school? Well that is to be expected. Has anyone sent you a mean electronic message? Oh my God, you have been cyberbullied!"

However, Willard said that something must be done to protect kids who truly are subjected to harassment online. "Nasty communications are likely commonplace online," Willard says. "Most are relatively mild situations that teens can handle. Sometimes these are very serious situations that are causing very significant harm. So we do have to address this situation effectively because some kids are truly being harmed."

School officials may be able to justify cyberbullying policies under a largely forgotten part of the *Tinker* case. The prominent part of *Tinker* is the substantial disruption or reasonable forecast of disruption language. But the language of Fortas's famous opinion also speaks of student speech "colliding with the rights of others" and as "an invasion of the rights of others."

The question becomes, when does a student's speech invade the rights of other students? The issue arose in *Harper v. Poway Unified School District* (2006) when school officials prohibited a student named Tyler Harper from wearing T-shirts with religious messages that criticized homosexuality. His shirts bore messages such as BE ASHAMED, OUR SCHOOL EMBRACED WHAT GOD HAS CONDEMNED, and HOMOSEXUALITY IS SHAMEFUL. He wore these shirts as an expression of his sincere religious beliefs.

However, the Ninth Circuit ruled 2–1 that school officials could prohibit Harper from wearing such shirts because they invaded the rights of gay and lesbian students. In the majority, Judge Steven Reinhardt reasoned that gay and lesbian students, an oppressed group, needed protection from intimidating speech. In dissent, Judge Alex Kozinski warned that "invasion of the rights of others" could effectively "overrule Tinker by granting students an affirmative right not to be offended."

If students believe they are being bullied online, school officials may be able to claim that they can restrict the offending students' speech because it invades the rights of others. There are no easy answers to this fraught issue, but the risk of restricting First Amendment rights for students is especially high in the cyberbullying discussion. Particularly when headline news stories show that students commit suicide after bullying, the impetus will only grow stronger to protect students from bullying and invasive conduct by others.

TEACHERS SUING STUDENTS

Perhaps an even more ominous development has occurred in some public schools, with teachers and administrators resorting to the judicial system to vindicate their own interests. Sometimes school officials may decline to assert authority over a student for off-campus online postings, perhaps fearing a lawsuit by the student and his or her parents testing the bounds of their authority, or that they may get no relief from the criminal justice system if it deems that the student online postings do not cross the line into the area of unprotected true threats.

But what if a student goes online and refers falsely to a teacher as a pedophile or a sex offender? Or the student goes online and creates a fake MySpace profile using the teacher's name? These incidents have occurred and have led to the unfortunate reality of some teachers and administrators filing defamation, invasion of privacy, and even negligent supervision claims against students and their parents.

Anna Draker, vice principal at Clark High School near San Antonio, sued two students after they allegedly defamed her on the Internet. Benjamin Schreiber and Ryan Todd falsely assumed Draker's identity and created a fake profile of her on MySpace. Schreiber and Todd posted a picture of Draker and pretended to be her when creating the MySpace profile. They falsely wrote that she was a lesbian and made several other false statements about her. Draker's Houston-based attorney, Murphy Klasing, described the statements as "four pages of filth."

In *Draker v. Schreiber*, Draker sued the students and their parents for defamation and for negligent supervision. She claims in her lawsuit that the parents are liable because they did not properly supervise their children's use of the Internet. As *San Antonio Express-News* columnist Ken Rodriguez wrote: "Draker's lawsuit will certainly spark debate on parental responsibility."

"I think what this [defamation suits by teachers] highlights to me is the lack of the ability [of] schools to discipline kids in any realistic way," said Klasing. "It means that when students do something that violates a civil statute or some common-law theory, the only other recourse is the legal system. You can't do much in the way of discipline in the schools, and if parents aren't disciplining, there is not much of an alternative other than the legal system."

The *Draker* case also has sparked debate over when student speech crosses the line from protected to unprotected speech. "It is hard to draw a real bright line between protected critical speech and defamation," acknowledged Klasing. "Students do have a right to criticize school officials but do not have a right to defame a person.

"Consider if a student says the principal is a jerk as opposed to saying the principal is a sex offender," he said. "There is a line somewhere between those two statements. I am certainly generally on the side of protecting speech, but you have to be able to punish someone for defamatory speech."

A trial court dismissed Draker's defamation suit, reasoning that the exaggerated statements were so preposterous in nature that a reasonable person would not believe that the students were asserting any real statements of fact. This finding harmed Draker's case because someone suing for defamation has to show that a defendant made a false statement of fact. Later, the trial court also dismissed her intentional infliction of emotional distress claim and other legal claims for the same reason. The Texas Court of Appeals upheld this decision in *Draker v. Schreiber* (2008).

Not all teachers or administrators fail in their defamation suits. In 1999, three teachers in Nobelsville, Indiana, sued a student and his mother for the student's online posting of material online claiming that the teachers were devil worshippers who should be shunned and mocked. The teachers' lawyer, Richard Darko, told the *New York Times*: "Threats and defamation don't have First Amendment protection." He explained to the Associated Press: "I think it's very unusual, extremely unusual for teachers to sue their students. . . . But at the same time, students are becoming more active in threatening and intimidating teachers and I think it's appropriate for them to respond the best way they can."

However, Ann Beeson, then a prominent cyber-liberties attorney with the ACLU, told the media: "It's a very sad day when teachers are suing for what is not only protected expression—even if it's juvenile expression—but for what I assume teachers experience all the time."

The Internet has become the leading First Amendment battleground for the last fifteen years. Much of this battle is being fought over and even by public school students who believe they should have the same level of free speech rights on the Internet as they do in the print medium. As more and more students use the Internet to express their frustrations with school administrators, teachers, and classmates, school disciplinary action will continue to increase. It is clear that this emerging area will remain one of the most fertile fields of First Amendment jurisprudence in the years to come. It's also clear that students must appreciate the significance of their online speech—that the Internet is not a special zone free from legal liability.

Many believe that the debates over Internet speech will be the forum where the U.S. Supreme Court once again wades into the troubled waters of student speech. In February 2010, the U.S. Court of Appeals for the Third Circuit decided two cases involving students who used MySpace to mock their principals. In two separate opinions, two different panels of judges reached different conclusions. At the time of this writing, the cases are before the full panel of the Third Circuit. Some believe they could go all the way to the Supreme Court.

Ken Paulson, president of the First Amendment Center, writes that students' increased use of social networking sites is "setting the stage for an eventual Supreme Court ruling that will decide how much free speech students in America's public schools really have."

If and when the Supreme Court does rule on student online speech, hopefully it will affirm that students do not shed their rights at this new First Amendment frontier any more than they do at the proverbial schoolhouse gate.

THE FRAGILE FUTURE

The battle for student' free speech rights rages on in a dizzying array of contexts. Cyberbullying, dress codes, book banning, true threats, and a host of other interesting issues will continue into the future, ensuring that free speech battles remain in the public eye.

A sampling of recent headlines confirms that this is a fertile area of dispute. Students in Baltic, South Dakota, put on "I Love Boobies" bracelets to raise awareness of breast cancer, but school officials consider them inappropriate. Students in Morgan Hill, California, wear American flag T-shirts on Cinco de Mayo. School officials prohibit the shirts, contending that the shirts would offend many Mexican American students. A student in Jackson, Mississippi, challenges school officials after they leave her photo out of the school yearbook; they refuse to allow her to be pictured wearing a tuxedo. The topics of controversy include tattoos, rosary beads, gay and lesbian T-shirts (both for and against), the distribution of religious literature, and even candy.

Uncertainty still abounds with respect to how far school authority should reach, when student speech constitutes a true threat or substantially disrupts or invades the rights of other students, and when student garb violates a dress code policy. School officials and student speech advocates spar over when schools have legitimate educational reasons to censor articles in student newspapers.

The questions are not entirely new. In the early twentieth century, courts grappled with controversies over whether Earl Wooster could criticize school officials before a student assembly and whether Pearl Pugsley could challenge a rule banning the wearing of lipstick and face powder. Peter Lander was punished in the nineteenth century for calling his teacher a name on the street. Today, students are punished for lampooning school officials on the information super-highway.

Some critics contend that many modern-day student messages such as "Bong Hits 4 Jesus," "Drugs Suck," and "International Terrorist" come across as either trivial or inappropriate, and those "juvenile expressions" might demean the grand purpose of the First Amendment. That view diminishes the reality that students are the future of the country and the future leaders of our constitutional democracy. These future leaders will not be able to appreciate the meaning of that democracy unless they live in an environment that fosters an appreciation of what the first freedom and the Bill of Rights mean.

Those critics misunderstand the reach of the First Amendment, which does not protect only the speech that we applaud, support, or laud. The history of free expression concerns speech that offends, criticizes, cajoles, and even hates. Justice William Brennan once wrote that "if there is a bedrock principle underlying the First Amendment, it is that the government may not prohibit an idea simply because it finds that idea offensive or disagreeable." While schools have the responsibility to teach students—as Chief Justice Burger said—"the boundaries of socially appropriate behavior," they also have the responsibility to protect and preserve their constitutional rights.

More than forty years ago, Justice Fortas wrote these words in his famous opinion in *Tinker*:

Any departure from absolute regimentation may cause trouble. Any variation from the majority's opinion may inspire fear. Any word spoken, in class, in the lunchroom, or on the campus, that deviates from the views of another person may start an argument or cause a disturbance. But our Constitution says we must take this risk, and our history says that it is this sort of hazardous freedom—this kind of openness—that is the basis of our national strength and of the independence and vigor of Americans who grow up and live in this relatively permissive, often disputatious, society.

Hopefully, most students in the future will go to schools where the real meets the ideal, where officials respect and promote tolerance for different opinions, where debate and discussion triumph over control and censorship. Hopefully, school officials will punish student speech where it is disruptive, not simply because of "undifferentiated fear."

Not the entire onus lies with school officials. Part of the responsibility lies with students themselves. Students must appreciate that with rights come responsibilities. The First Amendment has never been interpreted to protect all forms of speech—even for adults in a free society. Adults do not have a right to defame others, traffic in obscenity, or incite imminent lawless action. When students defame, threaten, or disrupt the classroom, they cannot reasonably expect protection from the Bill of Rights.

The history of free expression shows that the state of student speech is not static. It varies, changes, and evolves. This requires vigilance on the part of those committed to the First Amendment and on the part of students themselves. Free speech advocate and former student litigant Joseph Frederick warns that "if the youth do not learn how to use the First Amendment, they will lose it."

Many students learn too little about the First Amendment and the Bill of Rights—other than the fact that censorship is alive and well. American Bar Association president Stephen N. Zack wrote in the September 2010 issue of the *ABA Journal*: "Today there is significantly less understanding and appreciation of our Constitution and its role in preserving freedom. Civic education courses have become electives in some schools; at others they are not offered at all. We are producing a generation of citizens who are ill-equipped to govern themselves as participants in our democracy. We must do better."

The history of student expression shows that there is much we can do better.

ACKNOWLEDGMENTS

I would like to thank Helene Atwan, director of Beacon Press, and Chris Finan, president of the American Booksellers Foundation for Free Expression, for giving me the opportunity to write on the subject of student free speech rights for Beacon's vitally important series "Let the People Speak." I would also like to thank Allison Trzop, Crystal Paul, Susan Lumenello, and everyone else at Beacon who helped make this book a reality. I appreciated the effective editing of Allison, Helene, and others. I also want to thank Nikki Troia, my colleague at the First Amendment Center, for her proofreading and editing.

Thanks to the leadership and staff at the First Amendment Center for providing an environment and opportunity to write and speak about student free speech controversies through the years. It is a collegial atmosphere which I have appreciated greatly through the years. Thanks also to everyone I've worked with—particularly Janis Kyser, Maria Gallo, and Terry Morley—at the Center for Civic Education and the marvelous "We the People" program.

I send a special word of gratitude to everyone who spoke to me about student speech issues for this work, including John Tinker, Jeffrey Pyle, Christopher Eckhardt, Joseph Frederick, Russell Rieger, Douglas Mertz, Katy Dean, Jay Y. Rubin, Mark Goodman, John Bowen, Murphy Klasing, Gloria Olman, Jane Briggs-Bunting, and Henry Aronson. I'd like to thank Michigan State law professor Kristi Bowman for providing documents and pleadings from the "freedom button" cases in Mississippi. I'd also like to thank Paul Polidoro of the Watchtower Bible and Tract Society for providing a copy of Rosco Jones's article on his history.

Finally, I'd like to thank my parents for the educational opportunities and support they have provided through the years and my wife, Carla, for her unwavering encouragement and love.

NOTES

CHAPTER 1: NO RIGHTS FOR STUDENTS

Amar, Vikram David. "*Morse,* School Speech, and Originalism." *UC Davis Law Review* 42 (2009): 637.

Glass, Mary Ellen. *Earl Wooster: Memoirs of a Nevada Educator.* Reno, NV: Oral History Program of the University of Nevada, 1996.

CHAPTER 2: THE "FIXED STAR"

Ellis, Richard, Jr. *To the Flag: The Unlikely History of the Pledge of Allegiance.* Lawrence, KS: University of Kansas Press, 2005.

Hudson, David L., Jr. "Woman in Barnette Reflects on Famous Flag Salute Case." First Amendment Center (December 28, 2009), www.firstamend mentcenter.org/analysis.aspx?id=22441.

Jackson, Robert H. *The Struggle for Judicial Supremacy.* New York: Vintage, 1941.

Jones, Rosco. "Putting Kingdom Interests First," *Watchtower* (January 15, 1968): 57–62.

Leviton, Stuart. "Is Anyone Listening to Our Students? A Plea for Respect and Inclusion." *Florida State University Law Review* 21 (1993): 35.

Wright, Charles Alan. "My Favorite Opinion: The Second Flag Salute Case." *Texas Law Review* 74 (1996): 1297.

CHAPTER 3: BUTTONS AND ARMBANDS

Author interviews with Henry Aronson, Christopher Eckhardt, and John Tinker.

Bass, Jack. *Unlikely Heroes.* Tuscaloosa, AL: University of Alabama Press, 1990.

Bowman, Kristi L. "The Civil Rights Roots of *Tinker.*" *American University Law Review* 57 (2009): 1129.

Cohen, Tom. *Three Who Dared.* New York: Doubleday, 1969.

Hudson, David L., Jr. "On 30-Year Anniversary, Tinker Participants Look Back at Landmark Case." First Amendment Center (February 24, 1999), www .freedomforum.org/templates/document.asp?documentID=10386.

———. *The Silencing of Student Voices.* Nashville, TN: The First Amendment Center, 2003.

Johnson, John W. *The Struggle for Student Rights: Tinker v. Des Moines and the 1960s.* Lawrence, KS: University of Kansas Press, 1997.

Tinker, Mary Beth. "Foreword: Reflections on *Tinker*." *American University Law Review* 58, no. 5 (June 2009): 1120.

CHAPTER 4: A NEW ERA

Nelson, Jack. *Captive Voices: The Report of the Commission of Inquiry into High School Journalism in America.* New York: Schocken Books, 1974.

CHAPTER 5: SUPREME RETRACTIONS

Author interviews with Jane Briggs-Bunting, Katy Dean, Mark Goodman, Gloria Olman, and Russell Rieger.

Hudson, David L., Jr. "Cathy Cowan Reflects on Her High School Journalism Fight in *Hazelwood* Case," First Amendment Center (December 27, 2001), www.freedomforum.org/templates/document.asp?documentID=15516.

———. "Matthew Fraser Speaks Out on 15-Year-Old Supreme Court Free Speech Decision." First Amendment Center (April 17, 2001), www.freedom forum.org/templates/document.asp?documentID=13701.

Hudson, David L., Jr., and John E. Ferguson Jr. "The Court's Inconsistent Treatments of *Bethel v. Fraser* and the Curtailment of Student Rights." *John Marshall Law Review* 36 (2002): 181.

CHAPTER 6: BONG HITS

Author interviews with Joe Frederick and Douglas Mertz.

Foster, James C. *Bong Hits 4 Jesus: A Perfect Constitutional Storm in Alaska's Capital.* Fairbanks, AK: University of Alaska Press, 2010.

Starr, Kenneth W. "From Fraser to Frederick: Bong Hits and the Decline of Civic Culture." *UC Davis Law Review* 42 (2008): 661.

CHAPTER 7: COLUMBINE

Author interview with Jay Y. Rubin.

Calvert, Clay. "Free Speech and Public Schools in a Post-Columbine World: Check Your Speech Rights at the Schoolhouse Metal Detector." *Denver University Law Review* 77 (2000): 739.

Cullen, Dave. *Columbine*. New York: Twelve Publishing, 2009.

Hudson, David L., Jr. "Fear of Violence in Our Schools: Is 'Undifferentiated Fear' in the Age of Columbine Leading to a Suppression of Student Speech?" *Washburn Law Journal* 42 (2002): 79.

———. "Student Expression in the Age of Columbine: Securing Safety and Protecting First Amendment Rights." First Amendment Center, First Reports 6, no. 2 (September 2005), www.firstamendmentcenter.org/about.aspx?id=15858.

Pisciotta, Lisa M. "Beyond Sticks and Stones: A First Amendment Framework for Educators Who Seek to Punish Student Threats." *Seton Hall Law Review* 30 (2000): 635.

Roy, Lucinda. *No Right to Remain Silent: The Tragedy at Virginia Tech*. New York: Crown, 2009.

CHAPTER 8: THE DRESS DEBATE

Brunsma, David, and Kerry Rockquemore. "Examining the Effects of Student Uniforms on Attendance, Substance Use, Disciplinary Behavior Problems and Academic Achievement." *Journal of Educational Research* 92, no. 1 (1998): 53–62.

Murphy, Paul D. "Restricting Gang Clothing in Public Schools: Does a Dress Code Violate a Student's Right of Free Expression." *Southern California Law Review* 64 (1991): 1321.

U.S. Department of Education. *Manual on School Uniforms*, www2.ed.gov/updates/uniforms.html (first published 1996).

CHAPTER 9: THE NEW FRONTIER

Author interview with Murphy Klasing.

Curtis, Michael Kent. "Be Careful What You Wish For: Gays, Dueling High School T-Shirts, and the Perils of Suppression." *Wake Forest Law Review* 44 (2009): 431.

Hudson, David L., Jr. "Censorship of Student Internet Speech: The Effect of Diminishing Student Rights, Fear of the Internet and Columbine." 2000 *L. Rev. M.S.U.-D.C.L.* [*The Law Review of Michigan State University–Detroit College of Law*], 199, 219, 221 (2000).

———. "How Free Is Student Speech?" First Amendment Center (May 7, 2009), www.firstamendmentcenter.org//analysis.aspx?id=21525&SearchString=%27%27%27Fraser%27%27%27.

———. "Student Online Expression: What Do the Internet and MySpace Mean for Students' First Amendment Rights?" First Amendment Center (December 19, 2006), www.firstamendmentcenter.org/about.aspx?id=17913.

————. "Tinkering with *Tinker* Standards?" First Amendment Center (August 9, 2006), www.firstamendmentcenter.org/analysis.aspx?id=17253.

Servance, Renee. "Cyberbullying, Cyber-harassment, and the Conflict between Schools and the First Amendment." *Wisconsin Law Review*, vol. 2003, no. 6: 1213.

INDEX OF CASES